Code It
Yourself

WITHDRAWN

CODING
FROM SCRATCH

By Rachel Ziter

CAPSTONE PRESS
a capstone imprint

Coding from Scratch is published by Capstone Press
1710 Roe Crest Drive
North Mankato, Minnesota 56003
www.mycapstone.com

Library of Congress Cataloging-in-Publication Data is available on the Library of Congress website.

ISBN 978-1-5435-3589-1 (paperback)

Summary: Learn to create your own games, animation, presentations and musical projects in no time at all with Coding from Scratch. Whether you're just learning to code or need a refresher, this visual guide to coding will cover all the basics - coding tools, where to find them and how to use them - with hands-on, step-by-step instructions designed to make Coding from Scratch second nature.

Designer: Heidi Thompson

Photo Credits
Shutterstock: AlexZaitsev, Cover, Kotkoa, Cover, Phil's Mommy, 6
"Scratch is a trademark of Massachusetts Institute of Technology, which does not sponsor, endorse, or authorize this content. See scratch.mit.edu for more information."

Printed and bound in the United States of America.
529

CODING
FROM SCRATCH

Table of Contents

Musical Projects and Makey Makey

What Is Coding?

Playing with an app on your smartphone. Searching online. Clicking through a website. Without even realizing it, you're using coding. But as much as we use coding in our everyday lives, learning to code can still seem intimidating. Where do you start?

Let's begin with the basics: what is coding? Think of coding as the language used to communicate with a computer. By creating a set of code, you're writing directions in a language that the computer can follow. Although computers may seem super smart, that's not the case! The only reason computers know how to do anything is because they have been coded to do it. A computer's code—the very specific directions given by a person—allows it to be the super-smart device we all know and love.

The reality is, anyone can learn to code. In this book we'll be creating projects using one coding language in particular: Scratch.

TIP:

The projects in this book build in complexity. If you've never coded before, start with the first project and work your way through. If something doesn't make sense in a later project, try going back to earlier projects to find the answer.

Scratch is an online coding platform that uses colorful coding blocks to create everything from games to presentations to animation. The colored blocks are sorted into categories like Motion, Looks, and Sound. By connecting the colorful blocks, you can start coding whatever comes to mind. For example, if you want to code a character to move around and make noise, you would start with an Events block, then add a Motion block, and finish with a Sound block. (You can also use a Control block to make the events repeat as many times as you'd like.)

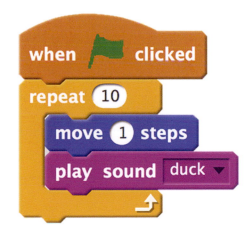

 Scratch runs on Adobe Flash Player, so before you do anything else, make sure your software is up-to-date. To download and install Flash go to: https://get.adobe.com/flashplayer/

Creating a Scratch Account

To create the projects in this book, you will need a Scratch account. Follow the steps below to get started!

1. Go to: www.scratch.mit.edu

2. In the upper right corner, click the *Join Scratch* button.

3. A window will pop up and ask you to create a Scratch username and password. Make sure not to use your last name as part of your username. Pick a password you can remember.

4. The next window will ask for your birth month and year. This is just to make sure you are old enough to use Scratch. If you are younger than 12, you will be asked for your parent's email to get permission to use Scratch.

Your responses to these questions will be kept private.
Why do we ask for this info ❓

Birth Month and Year	- Month - ▾	- Year - ▾
Gender	⭕Male ⭕Female ⭕	
Country	- Country -	▾

5. The next window will ask for an email address. Scratch will send one email—to confirm your email address—when you sign up. After that, you'll only get emails if you need to reset your password.

Enter your email address and we will send you an email to confirm your account.

Email address _____

Confirm email address _____

☐ Receive updates from the Scratch Team

6. The final screen will confirm that you have successfully signed up for Scratch and prompt you to check your email.

How to Use Scratch

Once you've created your Scratch account, you will see your username in the top right corner of the Scratch homepage. If you don't see your username, you need to sign in. Click *Sign In* and enter the username and password that you've created.

Press *Create* to start working on a new project.

If you've visited Scratch previously, click on this folder to access projects you've already started working on or finished.

You can also search other games and projects on Scratch. This can be a fun way to get inspiration for new projects and see all the possibilities of what can be created in Scratch! Try searching for a project similar to one you'd like to make, then open the existing project to see what code was used.

When you click *Create,* your screen will look like this:

TOOLS

These tools are found at the top of the screen. They are helpful for creating new projects. Click on the tool you want to use—it will turn blue and the mouse will turn into the tool. Then click on the item you'd like to duplicate, cut, grow, or shrink.

 stamp—The stamp is used to duplicate anything in your project. To use this tool, click on the icon so the cursor turns into the stamp, then click whatever you'd like to copy. You can click on a premade character or even a set of code.

 scissors—The scissors are used to delete items in your project.

 outward arrows—The arrows facing outward are used to grow characters. Continue clicking on the character until it is the desired size.

 inward arrows—The arrows facing inward are used to shrink characters. Continue clicking on the character until it is the desired size.

WHAT IS A SPRITE?

A sprite is any movable character or object used in a project. Sprites can be selected through the Scratch Library, created using drawing tools, or uploaded from the computer. Scratch Cat is an example of a sprite!

All sprites can be accessed in this box:

Sprite Library

NAME YOUR PROJECT HERE

This screen shows you what your project will look like when it's finished. In this area you can arrange your sprites on top of your background however you'd like for your project.

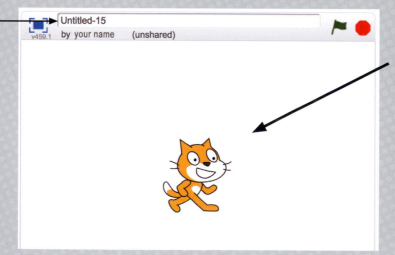

Untitled-15

by your name   (unshared)

v459.1

Scratch Cat will automatically appear on every project you start. He is the face of Scratch. If you don't want to use him in your project, it's OK! You can select whichever sprite you would like. But Scratch Cat will always appear with a new project to get you started.

SPRITE TOOLS:

 alien head—Click on the alien head to open the Sprite Library and select a sprite. All sprites are sorted alphabetically. You can choose anything from a dinosaur sprite to cheesy puffs to an airplane.

 paintbrush—Click on the paintbrush to open the paint tools and create your own sprite.

 folder—Click on the folder to upload an image from your computer to use as a sprite.

 camera—Click on the camera to use a picture from your computer as a sprite. A box will pop up asking to access the camera. Press *allow* to let Scratch access your computer's camera.

NAME YOUR SPRITE HERE

Click the blue ⓘ to open the sprite's information.

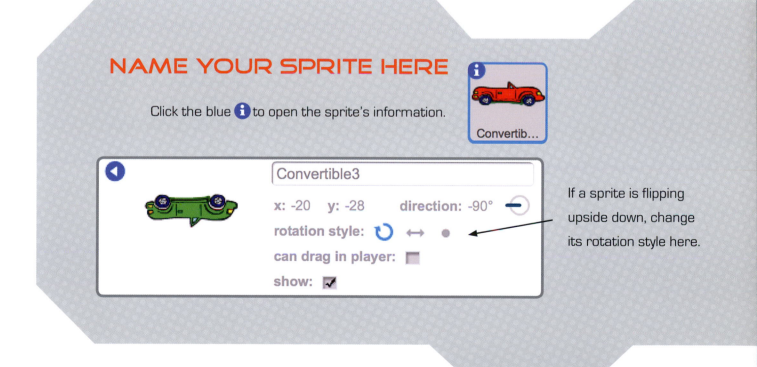

If a sprite is flipping upside down, change its rotation style here.

When you have selected a sprite, you will see three tabs in the top right corner: **Scripts**, **Costumes**, and **Sounds**.

Code blocks are color coded. To figure out which category a certain block is in, look at the color of the block and match it with the category.

SCRIPTS TAB:

The Scripts tab is the most important tab you will use in Scratch. This is where you will create the code for all your projects. When you click on the Scripts tab, you will have access to the different code blocks needed to create projects. The code blocks are grouped by category and color coded to make finding them easier.

Motion: These blocks are used to create movement. Using these blocks, you can tell your sprite to move around the screen, go to a particular place, turn, and more.

Looks: These blocks are all about appearance. Here you will find the code needed to make your sprite or project change colors, grow, shrink, swap backgrounds, switch costumes, and much more! You can even code your sprite to say or think certain things. (When you code it with a *say* block, a speech a bubble will appear above the sprite. The *say* and *think* blocks are here rather than in **Sound** because your sprite won't actually make any noise with these two blocks.)

Sound: Turn up the volume! The blocks in this category add sound to your sprites and/or background.

Pen: These blocks allow your sprites to draw lines wherever they move. (For example, if your sprite moves, then turns 90 degrees four times, you can create a square.) The size, color, and shade of the pen can also be programmed here.

Data: In this category you can create variables to use within your project. A variable is a value that can be changed throughout the course of a project. For example, you can use a variable for the number of lives a sprite has in a game. You could set the variable as "three" for the start of a game, and each time a sprite comes into contact with that variable, one life will be subtracted.

Events: The blocks in this category are some of the most important. These are your start commands. All code has a start command. This tells the program when it needs to start. These blocks will be the first piece used in any code you write. The most commonly used start command in this book will be the green flag.

Control: These blocks control how long certain things happen and if one thing causes another to start. There are repeat loops, wait commands, cloning blocks, and *if then* statements called conditional statements. (For example, *if* a sprite touches a certain color, *then* it needs to react in a certain way.) The *if then* conditional block will be one of the most used in this book.

Sensing: These blocks are used to detect things—like touching a certain sprite or color—in your code. They are often paired with the *if then* conditional block from Control. (For example, "If touching color blue, then the sprite jumps three times.")

Operators: These code blocks are used to combine codes or set a random range for something within a set of code. They will always be combined with other code blocks when used.

More Blocks: You won't see any blocks in this category at first—that's because you must create any blocks that go here. To see an example of a block being created and used in a project, check out the Ping Pong game!

In Scratch, code blocks snap together like puzzle pieces. Simply drag the blocks together to make them attach.

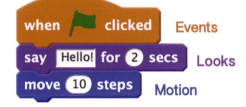

This code starts with the green flag being clicked. (This is the start command.) Next the sprite will say "Hello!" for two seconds. Once the two seconds have passed, the sprite will move 10 steps.

To take the blocks apart, you must pull from the bottom and down. If you remove a single piece, all the blocks attached below will stay connected to that piece. (You must pull each one off from the bottom.) Don't worry, you'll get the hang of it quickly! To throw away a block you no longer want or need, drag it back to the category you originally selected it from and let go.

The code you create will run in whatever order you place the blocks. Code begins at the top and works its way down. Order your code blocks in the order you want things to happen.

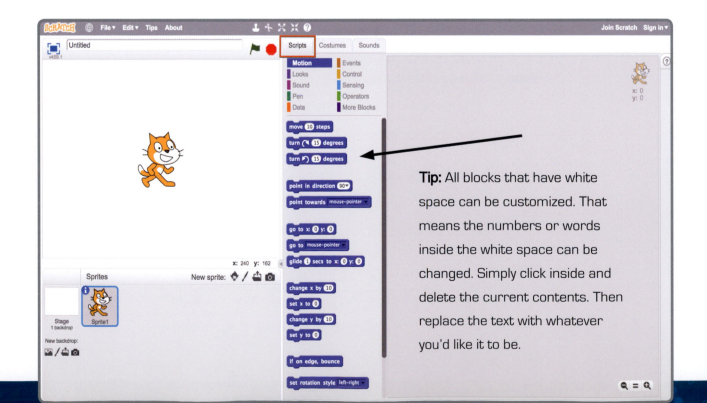

Tip: All blocks that have white space can be customized. That means the numbers or words inside the white space can be changed. Simply click inside and delete the current contents. Then replace the text with whatever you'd like it to be.

COSTUMES:

Here you can edit the appearance of the sprite you've chosen. You can also create your own sprite, or add a new costume to an existing sprite.

Different costumes can be used to make it look like a sprite is moving. Some sprites automatically come with more than one costume. For example, Scratch Cat has two costumes—his feet are in different positions in each costume. These costumes can be coded to make Scratch Cat look like he's walking. Multiple costumes are key to making your sprite look animated. Keep in mind that while you may have multiple costumes, there is still only one sprite!

When you open the Costumes tab, you will see tools you can use to customize your sprite. To learn more about the drawing tools, check out the guide on page 79.

You can name your costumes here. For this costume, we used the paint bucket to make Scratch Cat red instead of his usual orange.

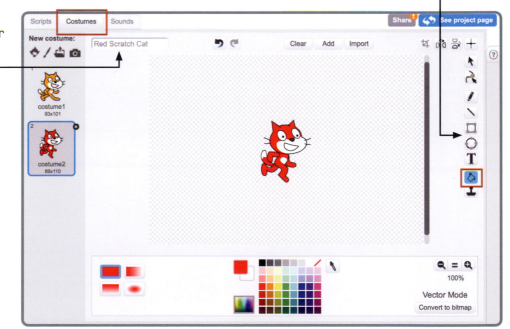

SOUNDS:

Once you've started a project, you can add sounds to your creation. To add a sound to a project, first select the sound from the library. You will later add it into the project through coding.

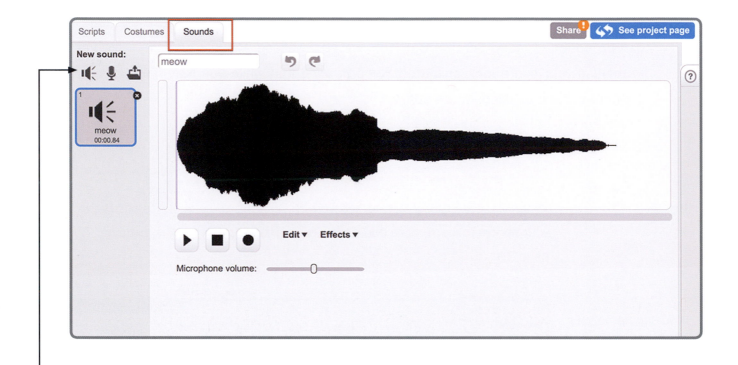

Each sprite comes with its own sound. Scratch Cat's sound is *meow*. Other sprites usually come with simple sounds like *pop*. Sprites that are imported or created using the graphic design tools do not have any sounds attached. To add a sound from the library, click on the speaker button.

SOUND LIBRARY:

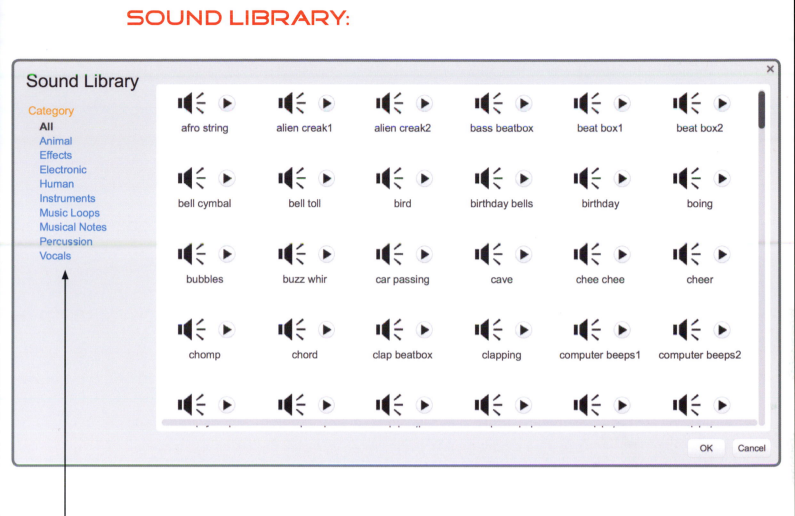

You can search for sounds easily by using the categories on the left side. The sounds within the library are sorted alphabetically to make them easier to find.

BACKDROPS:

Just like with sprites, there are lots of ways to access backdrops in Scratch and make them your own. You can select, create, upload, or snap a picture. The buttons used to create a new backdrop can be found on the bottom left corner of your screen, under the sprites section. There are four buttons you will use:

 mountain landscape—This icon opens the Backdrop Library so you can select a backdrop.

 paintbrush—This icon opens the paint tools, allowing you to create and name your own background.

 folder—This icon lets you to upload an image from your computer to use as a background.

 camera—This icon lets you to take a picture from your computer and use it as a background. (Note: When you click the camera, a pop-up box will ask to access the camera. Press *allow* to use the camera to create a backdrop.)

BACKDROP LIBRARY:

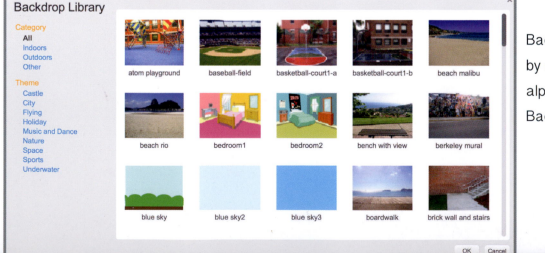

Backdrops are sorted by category and alphabetically in the Backdrop Library.

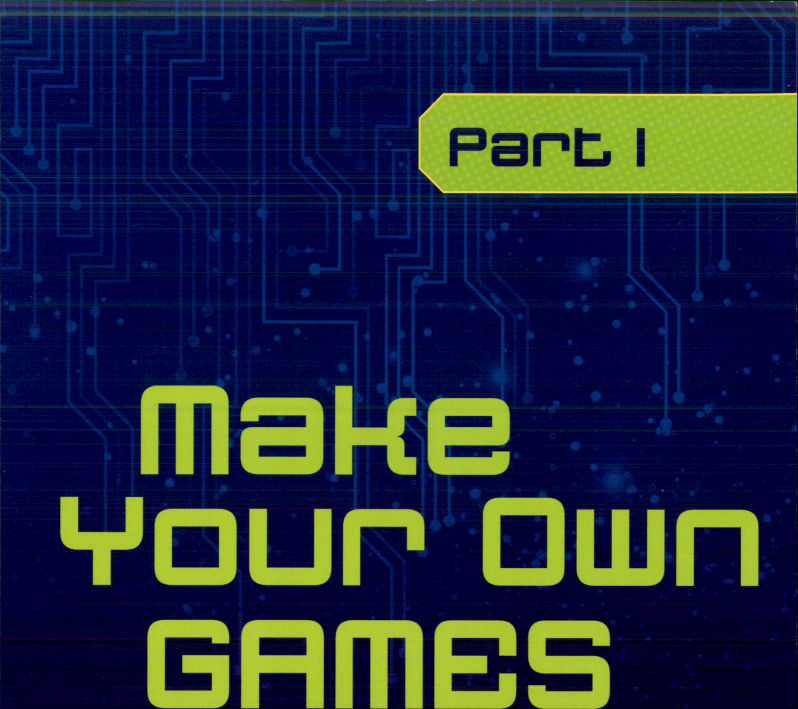

Part I

Make Your Own GAMES

What Makes a Game?

Although there are many different games out in the world to play, most games have the following factors in common:

Setting—Where does your game take place?

Goals—What task are you trying to complete by the end of the game?

Conditions—How do you win the game? How do you lose the game?

Mechanics—How does the main character make its way through the game?

Components—What are the different characters or objects in the game?

Rules—What can you do or not do in the game?

As you work through this book, try to identify the different parts of each game. When you've finished learning to code, you'll be able to create your own unique games. Keep the factors listed above in mind when inventing your own amazing original projects!

Keep your eye out for these game components in the projects to come!

Ready to get started? Take a look at this basketball court.

Try to identify all the factors found in the game of basketball.

*Answers on the next page

ANSWERS:

Setting—Basketball court

Goals—To score more points than the other team by the end of the allowed game time

Conditions—Earn points by throwing the ball successfully into the net to score points. If you score the more points than the other team in the allowed time, you win. If not, you lose.

Mechanics—To move around in the game, the character needs to run, jump, dribble, defend, and shoot the ball.

Components—Your teammates, the opposing team, the basketball hoop, the basketball, the referee

Rules—Shoot the ball into the net to score points. You can't move around the court without dribbling the ball at the same time—that's called traveling!

TRY ONE MORE TIME!

Identify the game components in this maze!

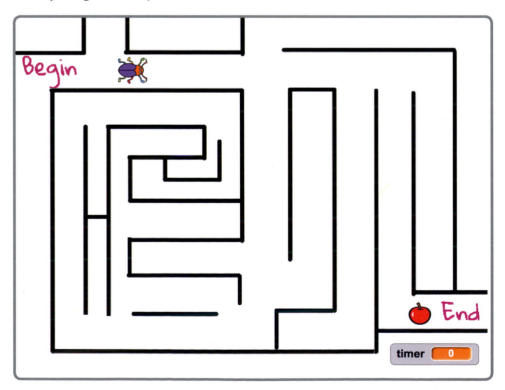

*Answers on the next page

ANSWERS:

Setting—Maze background

Goals—To get to the apple at the end of the maze

Conditions—To win, move through the maze and retrieve the apple. If you hit the black maze line, you lose.

Mechanics—Use the arrow keys to control the beetle and move around the maze.

Components—The main character will interact with the black maze and the apple as it moves through game.

Rules—Move through the maze using the arrow keys. Avoid touching the black maze wall or you'll be sent back to the beginning. Make it to the apple before the time runs out to win.

TIP:

The games in this section build on each other. You'll learn new skills in each game that you might need for future games, so resist the urge to jump ahead! If you get confused later on with a harder project, try looking back at an earlier game for help.

Race Game

HOW TO PLAY

Move your car sprites until one of them reaches the colored finish line at the end. You'll also learn how to edit your sprites' color and create your own background.

LET'S GET STARTED!

STEP 1: Log in to Scratch and click *create* to start a new project. Then select the scissors tool at the top of the screen and click on Scratch Cat to delete him. (You'll use a different sprite for this game.) Next click the alien head icon. This will open the Sprite Library. Click on the transportation category and select a car.

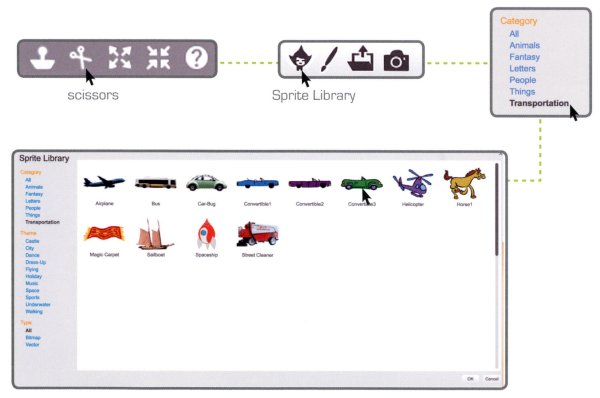

scissors

Sprite Library

Category
All
Animals
Fantasy
Letters
People
Things
Transportation

Sprite Library

Category
All
Animals
Fantasy
Letters
People
Things
Transportation

Theme
Castle
City
Dance
Dress-Up
Flying
Holiday
Music
Space
Sports
Underwater
Walking

Type
All
Bitmap
Vector

Airplane   Bus   Car-Bug   Convertible1   Convertible2   Convertible3   Helicopter   Horse1

Magic Carpet   Sailboat   Spaceship   Street Cleaner

OK   Cancel

OPTION: You can change the color of your race car using the paint bucket icon on the Costumes tab. Select the color you want from the color grid at the bottom of the page.

STEP 2: Click on the paintbrush icon under *New backdrop* to create your race backdrop. Name it *race* in the upper left-hand corner (on the opposite side of the screen).

paintbrush

TIP: Don't forget to name and save your project!

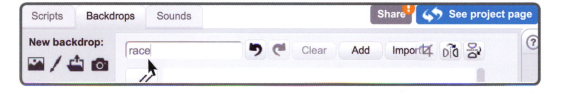

STEP 3: Use the drawing tools to create a race track with three lanes. When finished, it should look like this:

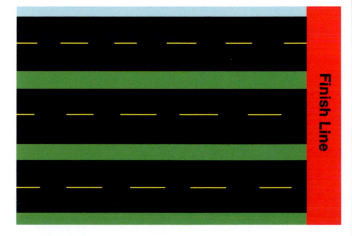

First use the paint bucket to fill in the background with green.

 Use the rectangle tool to draw three lanes on your road. Choose the black filled-in option at the bottom.

 Use the line tool to add one yellow line down the middle of each lane. Hold shift to make the line straight. (You can change the width so the line is thicker.)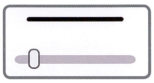

 Select a black line and change the width so it is thicker than the yellow line. Hold down shift to draw black lines through each of the yellow lines, creating the dashes on the road.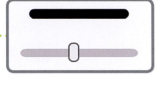

 Use the rectangle tool to create a red finish line at the end of the race. (Select the filled-in option and add it to the screen vertically, in the opposite direction of your lanes.)

 Use the text tool to type *Finish Line* and add the text box to your rectangle at the end. (Make sure your font is a different color than your finish line.) You will need to rotate the text box at the top so it sits vertically on top of the finish line.

 Last, but not least, use the paint bucket to make the sky above your race track blue.

STEP 4: Now that your car sprite and race track are created, you can start adding code. Click on the car sprite, then add the code shown here to its Scripts tab.

This code will be activated with the green flag.

This block causes the cars to start with an X coordinate of -200, making the cars start on the left of the screen.

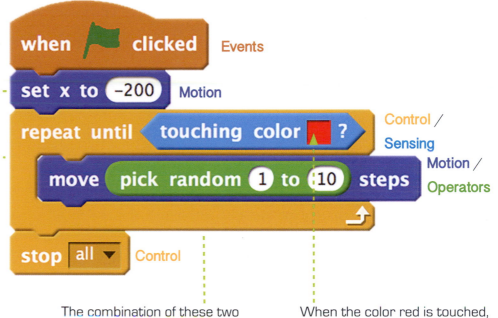

when [green flag] clicked — Events

set x to -200 — Motion

repeat until < touching color [red] ? > — Control / Sensing

move (pick random 1 to 10) steps — Motion / Operators

stop all ▼ — Control

Add a *repeat until* loop. The motion inside of the loop will continue until the sprite has touched the color red—the finish line!

The combination of these two blocks will cause your sprite to move at a random speed, which is needed in any race.

When the color red is touched, the sprite will stop moving and the race will end.

TOUCHING COLOR

To select the desired code for the color-sensing block, click inside the square. A small white finger cursor will appear. When the finger cursor appears, move the cursor to the color you'd like to select and click on it. The color you selected should now fill the square in the color-sensing block.

touching color [red] ?

STEP 5: Duplicate your car sprite twice using the stamp tool at the top of the screen. At the end of this step, you should have two exact copies of your sprite, along with the code that you programmed onto it.

 Find this tool at the top of the page. Click your car sprite twice to duplicate two times. You should now have a total of three sprites.

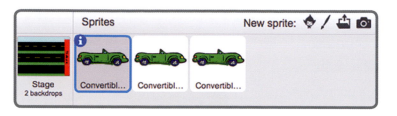

STEP 6: Go to the Costumes tab for the two new sprites you created and change their colors so they're no longer identical. (You want three separate cars so you can see which one wins the race!)

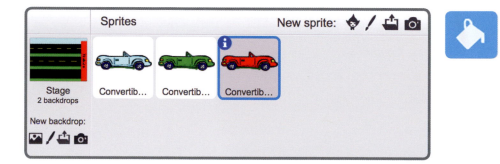

Fill in your sprites using the paint bucket so all the cars look different.

TIP:

Use the zoom symbol to get closer to the sprite. This will make it easier to fill in small areas, like the door handle.

STEP 7: Arrange the sprites on the background to the left of your screen. Then click the green flag to play and see which car wins!

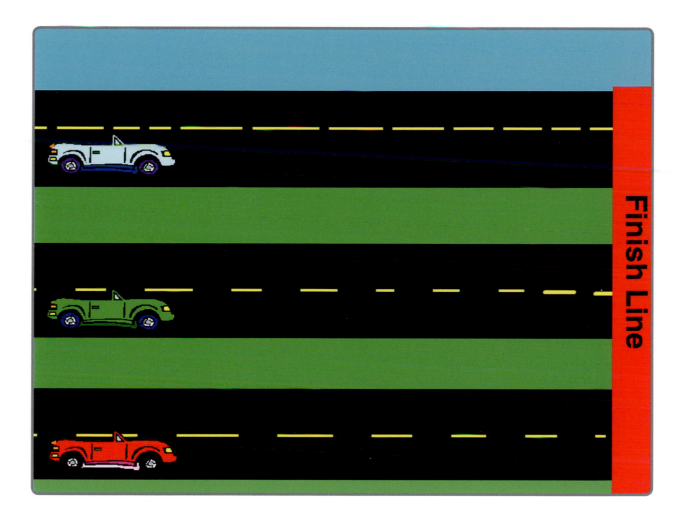

TIP:

Click on the blue square in the upper left corner of your screen to see your finished game in full-screen mode.

Use this link to see the finished game and watch the cars race toward the finish line:

https://scratch.mit.edu/projects/174138379/

Monkey Jumping on the Bed!

HOW TO PLAY

For this game you'll be working with the animal kingdom! Create and code a monkey sprite to move around randomly until he is caught. If he's caught, the backdrop will switch to a *game over* screen.

LET'S GET STARTED!

STEP 1: Click *create* to start a new project, then select the scissors at the top of the screen and click on Scratch Cat to delete him. Next click the alien head icon in the sprite panel and select the monkey from the Sprite Library. (You can narrow it down using the *Animals* category.)

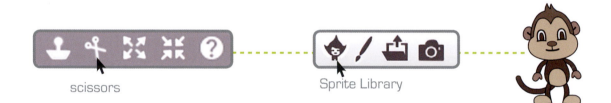

scissors   Sprite Library

STEP 2: In your backdrop panel, click on the mountain landscape icon and choose the bedroom background. This will automatically be saved as *bedroom1.*

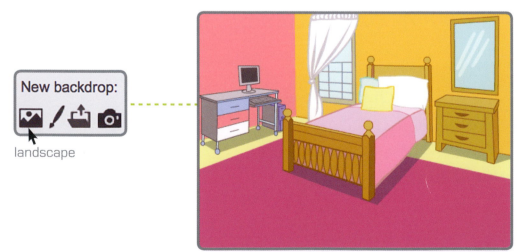

New backdrop:

landscape

STEP 3: Go to your backdrop tools and use the paintbrush to create a new backdrop. (This will be your *game over* screen.)

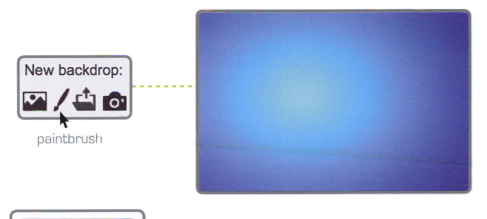

 paintbrush

winner   Name this backdrop *winner*.

 Use the paint bucket tool and, on the bottom right, select two colors to fill in the background with the dual-color effects. (Click on your blank backdrop to fill it with color.)

T Use the text icon and select the color black to type the winner message. Write whatever you want to appear at the end of your game. Use the sizing dots around the text to make it as large as you'd like.

STEP 4: Time to add sound! Select your monkey sprite. Then go to the Sounds tab.

Click on the speaker icon to open the Sound Library and select the *rattle* sound effect. [Remember, sounds are sorted alphabetically - - - - - - - to make it easier to find them.]

Use this dark gray bar to slide up and down through the different sounds. To preview the sound, click on the *play* button next to it. Click *OK* on the bottom right to select it.

Once your sound is selected, it should show under the Sounds tab, along with *pop*—the sound that automatically comes with most sprites. If the *rattle* sound isn't there, go back into the Sound Library and re-select it.

Note: Just because you select a sound on one sprite doesn't mean it automatically shows up on another sprite in your projects. Sounds must be selected for each sprite that needs noise.

STEP 5: Under the Scripts tab, add this code to your monkey sprite.

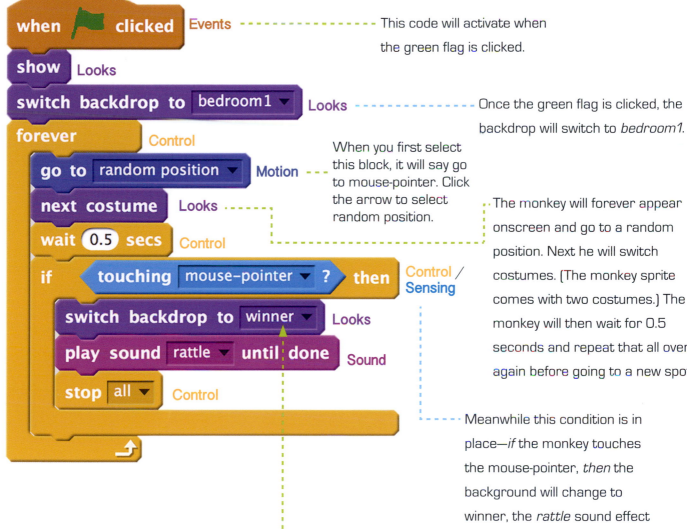

when ▶ clicked   Events - - - - - - - - - - - - - This code will activate when the green flag is clicked.

show Looks

switch backdrop to bedroom1 ▼ Looks - - - - - - - - - - - Once the green flag is clicked, the backdrop will switch to *bedroom1*.

forever Control

go to random position ▼ Motion - - - When you first select this block, it will say go to mouse-pointer. Click the arrow to select random position.

next costume Looks - - - - - -

wait 0.5 secs Control

if touching mouse-pointer ▼ ? then Control / Sensing

switch backdrop to winner ▼ Looks

play sound rattle ▼ until done Sound

stop all ▼ Control

The monkey will forever appear onscreen and go to a random position. Next he will switch costumes. (The monkey sprite comes with two costumes.) The monkey will then wait for 0.5 seconds and repeat that all over again before going to a new spot.

Meanwhile this condition is in place—*if* the monkey touches the mouse-pointer, *then* the background will change to winner, the *rattle* sound effect will play, and the game will stop.

If you can't find a background called *winner*, go back to your backdrops tab and be sure that you named it correctly.

You're finished! Click on *See project page* to play your game and try to catch the monkey. See the finished game here:

 See project page

https://scratch.mit.edu/projects/154122791/

Save Scratch Cat!

HOW TO PLAY

Code Scratch Cat to fall from a random spot in the sky in hopes that a bat will catch him and carry him to safety. If Scratch Cat falls without the bat catching him, the game is over. If the bat catches Scratch Cat and brings him to the safe button, he is saved!

LET'S GET STARTED!

STEP 1: Start a new project—don't forget to name it! Then click on the mountain icon to open the Backdrop Library. Select the *woods* backdrop.

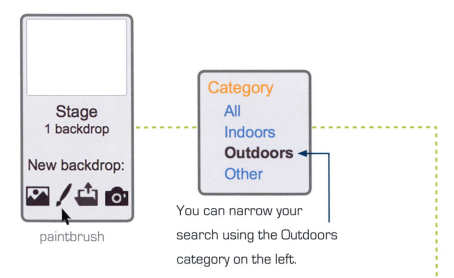

paintbrush

You can narrow your search using the Outdoors category on the left.

Once you have selected the correct backdrop, go to the Backdrops tab and add a small, filled-in rectangle to the bottom of your screen. Make this rectangle pink. (Once you get the hang of coding, feel free to use any color not in the background or on any of your sprites. The sprite colors are orange, black, and brown.)

Make sure to choose the filled-in rectangle icon!

STEP 2: Use the paintbrush to create two new backdrops. You'll need a *winner* backdrop and a *game over* backdrop.

paintbrush

Name both backdrops in the box at the top left.

winner   game over

Use the paint bucket to fill in both backdrops with your desired color(s).

T Use the text tool to type your winning and losing messages on the correct backdrops.

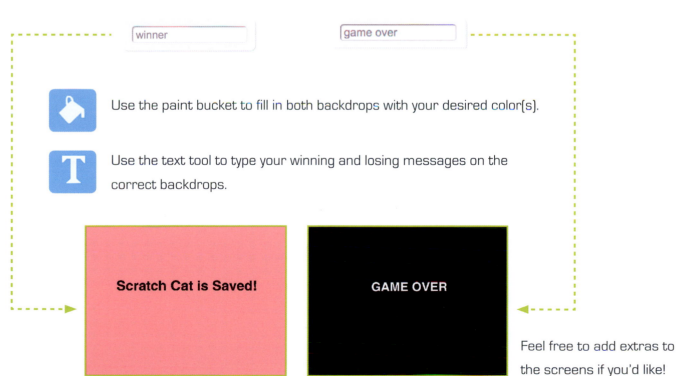

Scratch Cat is Saved!   GAME OVER

Feel free to add extras to the screens if you'd like!

STEP 3: Leave Scratch Cat on the project; you will be using him as a sprite. Open the Sprite Library and select a bat sprite and a button sprite. (You can find these in the *Animals* and *Things* categories.) You should now have three sprites. In the button sprite's information section, name it *safe button*.

Sprite Library

Note: If you'd like to save a sprite other than Scratch Cat in this game, now is the time to make the switch. All code placed on Scratch Cat in these directions will need to go on the new sprite you've selected if you wait till the end!

STEP 4: Click on the button sprite, then open the Costumes tab to customize it. Use the text tool to add the word *safe* to the button sprite. Feel free to change the button's color using the paint bucket. Once you're finished, drag it to the safe spot of your choice in your game!

STEP 5: Click on the Scripts tab and add the below code to the button sprite. Remember to match the code blocks to the correct category using their color.

Scripts   Costumes   Sounds

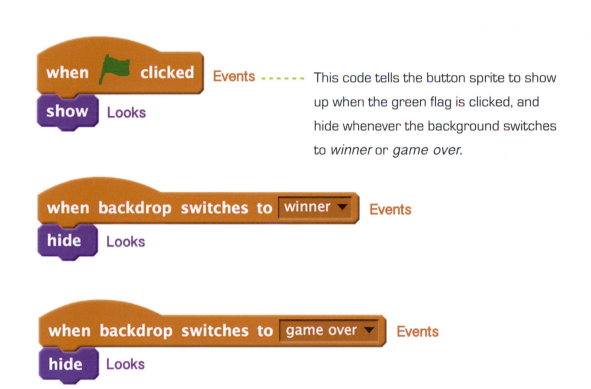

when ⚑ clicked   Events ------ This code tells the button sprite to show up when the green flag is clicked, and hide whenever the background switches to *winner* or *game over*.

show   Looks

when backdrop switches to winner ▼   Events

hide   Looks

when backdrop switches to game over ▼   Events

hide   Looks

STEP 6: Select the bat sprite, and add the four code blocks you see below to its Scripts tab.

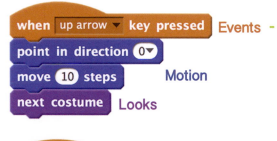

Scripts   Costumes   Sounds

```
when up arrow ▼ key pressed    Events
point in direction 0▼
move 10 steps                  Motion
next costume   Looks
```

These code blocks will activate when one of the arrow keys is pressed. The bat will then point in the appropriate direction, move, and switch costumes.

```
when left arrow ▼ key pressed
point in direction -90▼
move 10 steps
next costume
```

To select which arrow key will move the bat, find the below block in **Events**. It will say *space key* at first. Click the arrow to open the drop-down menu and select the correct key.

```
when right arrow ▼ key pressed
point in direction 90▼
move 10 steps
next costume
```

```
when space ▼ key pressed
```

To select which direction the bat will move, find the below block in **Motion**. (The drop-down menu will help you understand which number represents which direction.)

```
when down arrow ▼ key pressed
point in direction 180▼
move 10 steps
next costume
```

```
point in direction 90▼
```

The costume block is used to make the bat look like it's flapping its wings. It will change between these two costumes as it moves. (Both costumes come with the bat sprite.)

STEP 7: Finish the bat by adding these last few blocks of code to its Scripts tab.

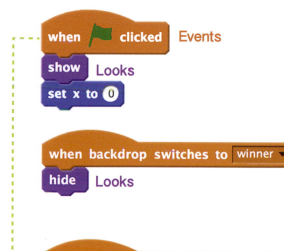

These codes make the bat appear when the green flag is clicked, then set its X coordinate to 0 (the center of the screen) at the start of the game, and hide on the *winner* and *game over* screens.

Use the drop-down menu to select the option you need.

Imagine your Scratch work space is a big coordinate plane.

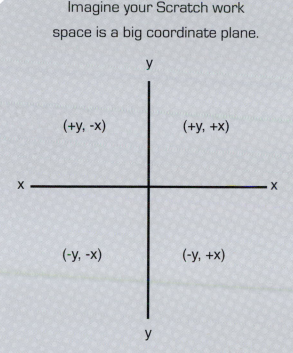

Changing the X and Y in the **Motion** block refers to the X and Y axis of a coordinate plane. If you have a positive Y coordinate, it will be found on the upper half of the plane. If you have a negative Y coordinate, it will be found on the lower half. If you have a positive X coordinate, it will be found on the right side. If you have a negative X coordinate, it will be found on the left side.

A **quadrant** is any of the four quarters into which something is divided by two real or imaginary lines (in this case, the X and Y axes) that intersect each other at right angles.

As you move your mouse around the plane, the X and Y coordinates on the bottom will change to show the mouse coordinates. X:0 Y:0 indicates that you are in the middle of the screen or coordinate plane. This is called the **origin**.

STEP 8: Click on your Scratch Cat sprite and add this code to his Scripts tab.

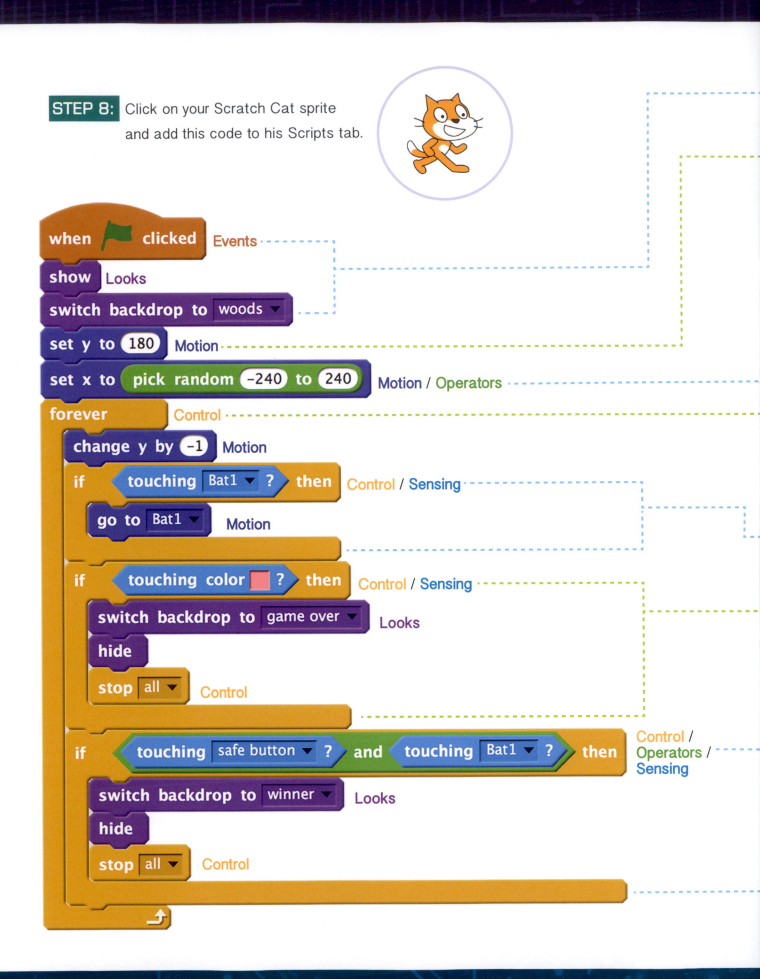

when 🚩 clicked — Events

show — Looks

switch backdrop to woods

set y to 180 — Motion

set x to pick random -240 to 240 — Motion / Operators

forever — Control

    change y by -1 — Motion

    if touching Bat1 ? then — Control / Sensing

        go to Bat1 — Motion

    if touching color ⬛ ? then — Control / Sensing

        switch backdrop to game over — Looks

        hide

        stop all — Control

    if touching safe button ? and touching Bat1 ? then — Control / Operators / Sensing

        switch backdrop to winner — Looks

        hide

        stop all — Control

When the green flag is clicked, Scratch Cat will appear and the background will change to the woods backdrop.

Scratch Cat will set his Y coordinate to 180 so he starts at the top of the screen. (The Y coordinate is the position along the Y axis, which runs up and down. 180 is the highest Y position on the Scratch grid.)

Scratch Cat's X coordinate is set to random -240 to 240 so he falls from a different spot on the X axis each time the game is played. (The X coordinate is the position along the X axis, which runs left to right. -240 to 240 is the X coordinate range for the Scratch window.) The bottom section of code is held inside a forever loop. That means it will repeat continuously throughout the game. The Y coordinate will change by -1, causing Scratch Cat to fall downward. (To make him fall faster, change the number to a more negative number, like -2 or -3.)

There are three different conditions—*if thens*—that can happen to Scratch Cat. To code what happens if a condition is met, the code blocks go inside the loop of the *if then* block.

1. The **first condition** tells Scratch Cat that *if* he touches the bat, *then* he should move wherever the bat does. (This **Motion** block will originally say *Go to mouse pointer*; select *Bat1* in the drop-down bar.)

2. The **second condition** says that *if* Scratch Cat touches the pink rectangle at the bottom of the screen, *then* the screen will switch to game over, Scratch Cat will hide, and everything will stop.

3. The **final condition** says that *if* the bat reaches the safe button with Scratch Cat, *then* the background will switch to the *winner* backdrop and stop all. (To select both the safe button and the bat, you will need to select the *and* block from **Operators** and both sprite blocks from **Sensing**. Try building this block separately before dropping it into your **Control** block.)

TIP:
See page 29 for a reminder on how to select the correct color in your **Sensing** block.

Use this link to check out the finished game and try your luck at saving Scratch Cat:
https://scratch.mit.edu/projects/158576405/

How Did the Crab Cross the Road?

HOW TO PLAY

Use the arrow keys to move your crab across a busy street without getting hit by a car. If the crab is hit, you'll be sent back to the beginning. If the crab makes it safely across the street, you win!

LET'S GET STARTED!

STEP 1: Start a new project. Use the scissors to delete Scratch Cat, then open the Sprite Library. Select the crab sprite and a car sprite.

scissors   Sprite Library

STEP 2: Click on the paintbrush icon in the backdrop tools to draw your own road background that looks like what you see here:

New backdrop:

paintbrush

 Use the filled-in rectangle to make the lanes.

 Use the line tool to make the lines on your road.

*For more specific instructions on creating your road, check out step 3 in Race Game!

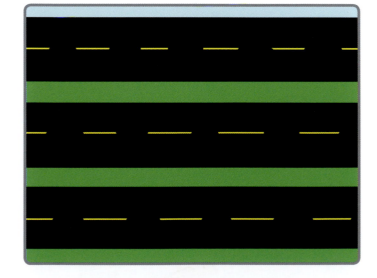

STEP 3: Add the code blocks you see below to your crab sprite.

These **Motion** and **Events** blocks control which direction the crab moves and by how much.

when up arrow ▼ key pressed Events
change y by 10 Motion

when left arrow ▼ key pressed
change x by -10

when right arrow ▼ key pressed
change x by 10

when space ▼ key pressed
change y by -10

STEP 4: Add the following code to the car sprite. This will create a screen scrolling effect in your game.

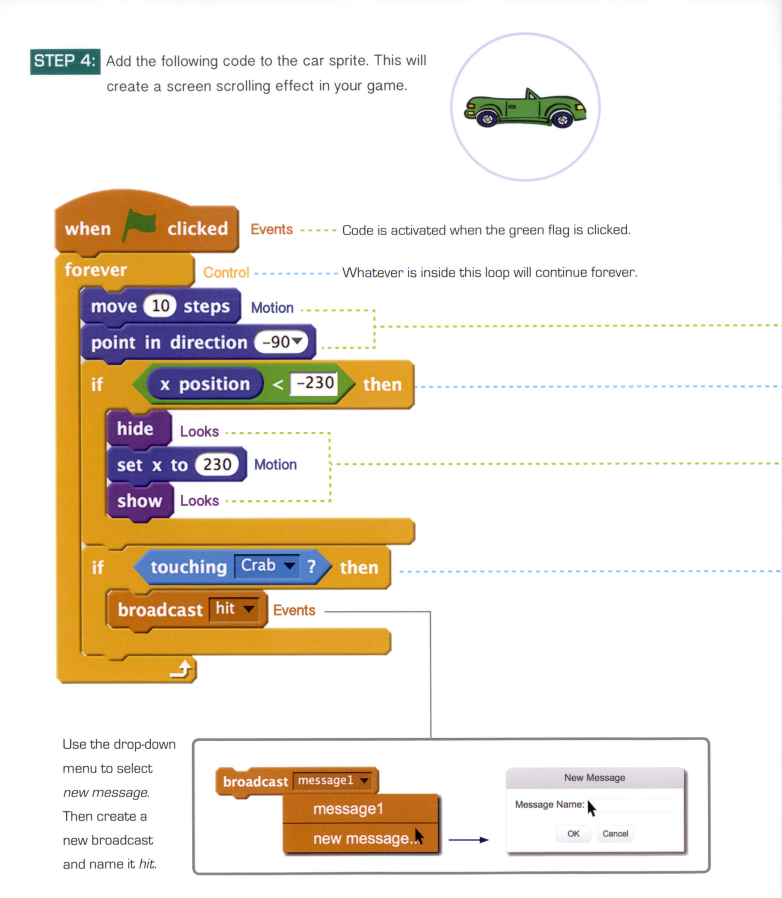

when [green flag] clicked — Events ---- Code is activated when the green flag is clicked.

forever — Control --------- Whatever is inside this loop will continue forever.

move 10 steps — Motion ....

point in direction -90▼ ....

if ⟨ x position < -230 ⟩ then

hide — Looks ....

set x to 230 — Motion ....

show — Looks ....

if ⟨ touching Crab ▼ ? ⟩ then

broadcast hit ▼ — Events

Use the drop-down menu to select *new message*. Then create a new broadcast and name it *hit*.

broadcast message1 ▼
  message1
  new message...

New Message

Message Name: |

OK   Cancel

These two blocks will make the car move at a certain speed and to the left. That is the direction the screen scrolling code is also going. (Use a number larger than five in the first block to make the car go faster.)

Combine the inequality block from **Operators** and the X-position block from **Motion** to create this block. (Try combining them separately and then dragging them into your **Control** block.)

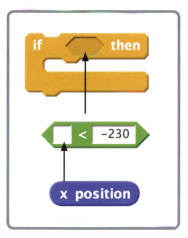

The combination of blocks inside the *if then* conditional statement will keep the car moving until the condition—*X position < -230*—has been met. (Note: -230 is the edge of the *X* axis. If the car kept moving beyond that, we wouldn't be able to see it!) If the car reaches an X coordinate less then -230, the sequence of code inside the loop will start. If the car reaches -230, we need it to hide, reposition itself onto the other side of the screen, and reappear. This creates the illusion of the car scrolling through the screen.

This conditional statement is activated when the car sprite touches the crab sprite. Whenever this happens you broadcast—send a message—to the crab telling it that it has been hit. (We will code what happens to the crab in another step.)

STEP 5: Change the rotation style of the car sprite so it doesn't flip upside down when it moves. To do this, click on the small letter 🛈 to open the sprite's information. Then click the side-to-side arrow in rotation style.

STEP 6: Once you have changed the rotation style, use the stamp tool to duplicate the car sprite twice. (You should now have a total of three cars.) In the Costumes tab, use the paint bucket to change the cars' colors so they don't all look the same. (Go back to Race Game if you need help.)

STEP 7: Add the below code to your crab sprite. This tells the crab to react to the *hit* message it will receive when the car touches it. (Use the drop-down menu in the **Events** block to select the correct option.)

STEP 8: Arrange the sprites on the screen as shown on the next page. (You may need to use the shrink tool to fit the sprites on the screen.)

shrink tool

To use the shrink tool, click on the inward-arrows icon, then continue clicking the sprite you'd like to shrink until it's the correct size.

Stagger the car sprites along the lanes on the road so they move across the screen at different times.

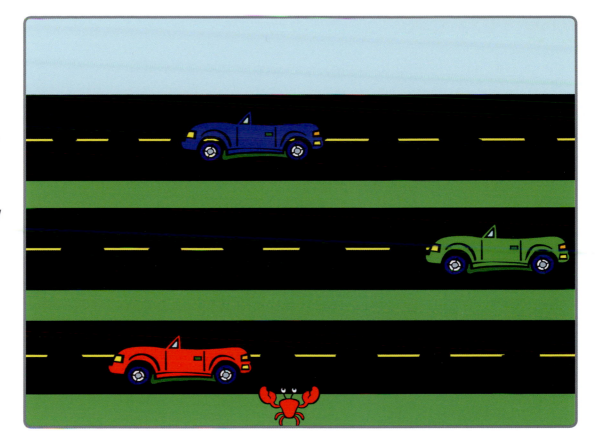

To change the car speeds, edit the **Motion** block in the code.

`move 10 steps`

TIP:
You do not need to change the numbers on the **Motion** block when you drag it out from the selection area. The coordinates will update when you move the sprite. (It's okay if exact location of your crab is different from what you see here. Yours may be placed at a different location than the one shown.)

↺ **See project page** Click on *See project page* to play. Use the arrow keys to move your crab across the road. Don't get hit! Use this link to check out the finished game: https://scratch.mit.edu/projects/174141026/

Space Muffins

HOW TO PLAY

Use the up and down arrows to control a spaceship that is trying to destroy invading dinosaurs. To destroy the dinosaurs, click the space bar to blast muffins at them!

LET'S GET STARTED!

STEP 1: Open a new project and use the scissors to delete Scratch Cat. (Don't forget to name your project!) Then choose a spaceship, a muffin, and a dinosaur sprite from the Sprite Library.

scissors   Sprite Library

STEP 2: Use the paintbrush in your backdrop toolbar to create a new backdrop.

paintbrush

 Name your new backdrop *space*.

 Use the paint bucket to color the background black. Then use the paintbrush to add white stars. (You'll need to increase the paintbrush's thickness.)

STEP 3: In the spaceships' Costumes tab, delete the *spaceship-b* costume by clicking the *x* in the upper right corner. Then duplicate the *spaceship-a* costume by clicking on the stamp tool at the top of your screen, then on the *spaceship-a* costume.

Change the first costume's name to *spaceship*. Then convert the second costume to bitmap mode by clicking *Convert to bitmap* at the bottom right of the screen. Use the grabber tool in the toolbar on the left to pull apart pieces of the ship. (You need to draw a box around each part of the spaceship you want to break apart and then drag it.) Name the second costume *crash*.

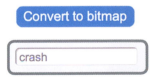

grabber tool

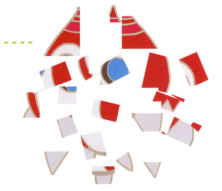

BITMAP MODE VS. VECTOR MODE

There are two different drawing modes in Scratch: **bitmap** and **vector**. Bitmap mode makes it easy to fill in backgrounds and shapes and is good for simple uses. However, in bitmap mode, you won't be able to resize or reshape anything you make. The drawing tools in vector mode are similar to tools in bitmap mode. However, in vector mode you can create another shape and still go back to a previous one and move it. In this mode, you can also reshape objects that you have made.

STEP 4: Arrange the spaceship sprite on the background as shown below. Be sure to shrink the sprites to the right sizes using the shrink tool. (The muffin should be about half the size of the spaceship.)

shrink tool

To rotate the spaceship, click on the ⓘ to open the sprite's information. Turn the line on the direction circle until the ship is facing to the right.

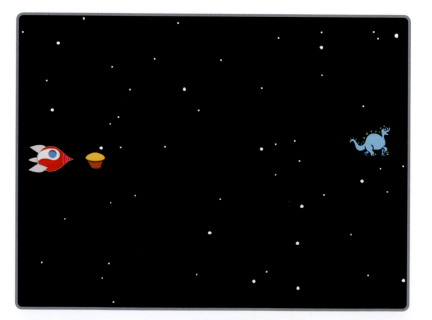

STEP 5: Go to the Sounds tab for the spaceship sprite and open the Sound Library. Select the *cymbal crash* effect. Then add the below code to your spaceship sprite's Scripts tab.

| Scripts | Costumes | Sounds |

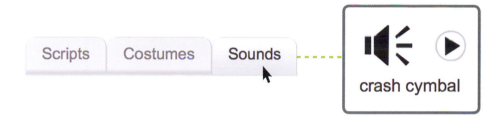

crash cymbal

when up arrow **key pressed** — Events

change y by 10 — Motion

when down arrow **key pressed**

change y by -10

This will tell the spaceship to move up or down with the arrow keys.

This block tells the spaceship that when the green flag is clicked, the spaceship's costume will switch to the intact spaceship. Then the ship will start in the middle of the Y axis (0).

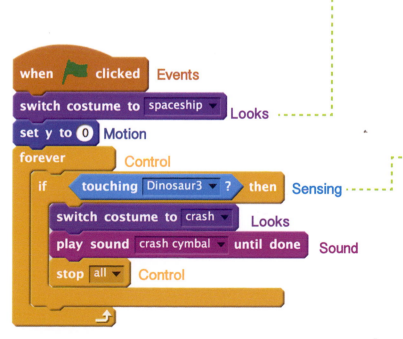

when 🏳 **clicked** — Events

switch costume to spaceship — Looks

set y to 0 — Motion

forever — Control

if touching Dinosaur3 ? **then** — Sensing

switch costume to crash — Looks

play sound crash cymbal **until done** — Sound

stop all — Control

There is one condition on the spaceship, saved within the forever loop. If the spaceship touches the dinosaur, the ship's costume will change to *crash*, the *cymbal crash* sound will play, and the game will stop. (The *stop all* code stops other codes in the game, like the dinosaurs invading.)

WHAT IS THE CLONING CODE BLOCK?

Before we go further, let's talk about the cloning block. You'll need it for the muffin and dinosaur sprites. If you preview the game using the link at the end, you'll notice that multiple dinosaurs invade and multiple muffins are blasted out. But so far, we have only one dinosaur and one muffin.

So how do you get from here to there? That's where the cloning block comes in. A clone is a copy of an existing sprite. Using code, you can tell your sprite(s) when to make a clone and give specifics on what you need that clone to do. The cloning blocks can be found in the Control category.

These blocks will be used in the next few parts of code:

LET'S GET CLONING!

To make multiple clones, pair the *create clone* block from Control with a forever loop or a repeat loop (also in the Control category) to create the desired number of clones.

STEP 6: Click on your muffin sprite, then open the Sounds tab. Open the Sound Library and select *laser2*. Then add the code blocks below to the muffin sprite.

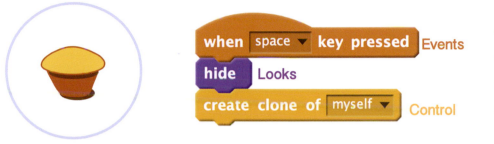

When the space bar is clicked, the original sprite will hide, and the muffin sprite will create a clone.

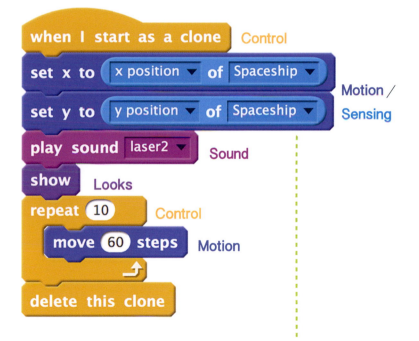

This code tells the muffin sprite that when it starts as a clone, its X and Y coordinates should be the same as those of the spaceship sprite. This will make it look like the muffin is blasting from the ship. Then the *laser2* sound will play, and the muffin will show, move across the screen, and disappear. (To make the muffin move faster or slower, change increase or decrease the number in the *move __ steps* **Motion** block.)

Use the **Sensing** and **Motion** blocks to create the *set X to* and *set Y to* part of the spaceship code. Select the correct entry from the drop-down menu and drag it inside the *set X to* or *set Y to* code block. Then you can drag the complete block into place within your larger code block.

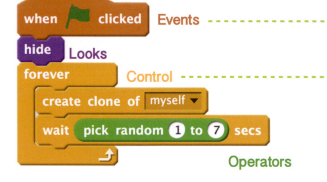

This code starts when the green flag is clicked.

The original sprite will hide, and the dinosaur will create a clone every 1–7 seconds. (This will happen forever thanks to the forever loop.) The wait allows the dinosaurs to come out at random times throughout the game.

This code tells the cloned dinosaur sprites what to do when they are created. Once cloned, they must go to the far right of the screen (X=240). Then their color will be set to something random—this makes each dinosaur come out a different color.

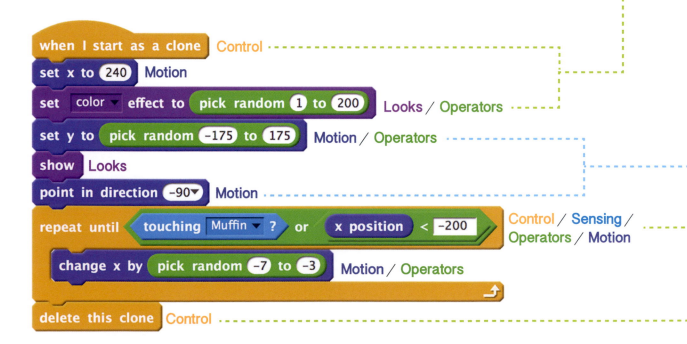

The clone must then set its Y coordinate to random location between -175 and 175. (This means the dinosaur will enter the screen at a random spot on the Y axis.) Then it will show and point to the left of the screen (-90). To create the *set Y to random* block, use the *set Y block* from **Motion** and the *pick random* block from **Operators**.

Then the dinosaur will change its X by a random number from -7 to -3. This controls how fast the dinosaur invades. The dinosaur will repeat this random change until it has touched the muffin or its X position is less than -200. (An X position of less than -200 means the dinosaur has passed the spaceship on the screen.) When either one of those things happen, the clone will delete.

Drag these blocks (**Sensing**, **Operators**, and **Motion**) together to make the big block. Then drag it inside the forever loop from the **Control** category.

STEP 8: Click on your backdrop and open the Sounds tab. Select the *space ripple* sound. Then go to the Scripts tab and add this final code.

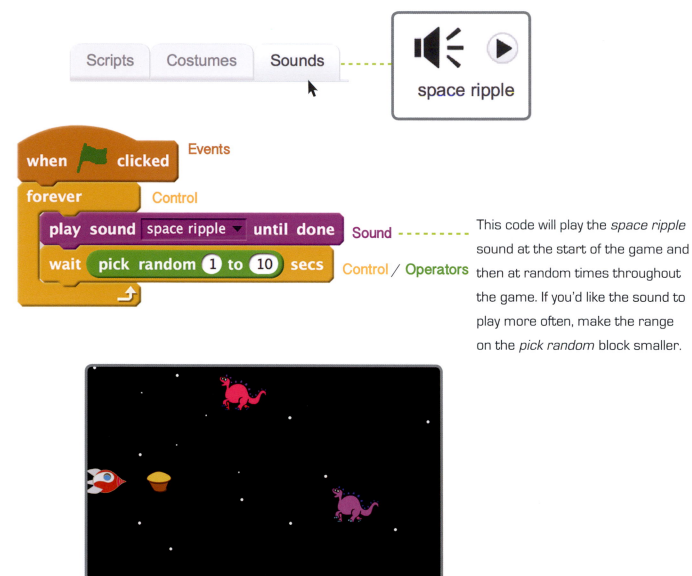

This code will play the *space ripple* sound at the start of the game and then at random times throughout the game. If you'd like the sound to play more often, make the range on the *pick random* block smaller.

Click on the green flag to play your game. Use the arrow keys to move your spaceship and avoid the dinosaurs. Use the space bar to blast muffins at the dinosaurs before they destroy your ship! Use this link to see the finished game:

https://scratch.mit.edu/projects/178325240/

HOW TO PLAY

Use the arrow keys to move a red ball through a maze you've created. While moving through the maze, avoid the blue ball—if you touch it, you'll be sent back to the beginning! Try to make it to the yellow ball at the end of the maze before the timer runs out.

LET'S GET STARTED!

STEP 1: Start a new project and delete Scratch Cat. (Don't forget to name your project!) Then select the ball sprite from the Sprite Library.

Sprite Library

Use the stamp tool to duplicate your ball twice. You should now have three ball sprites. Go into the Costumes tab of each ball and use the paint bucket to change the colors so you can tell them apart. Then go into each sprite's information and name it according to color.

Think about which ball you want to do what. In this example, the red ball will be moving through the maze. The blue ball will be moving around the maze trying to stop the red ball. The yellow ball will act as the end goal.

STEP 2: Use the paintbrush icon to create a new backdrop.

New backdrop:

paintbrush

winner   Name the background *winner.*

 Use the paint bucket tool and mix teal and white to create this backdrop effect.

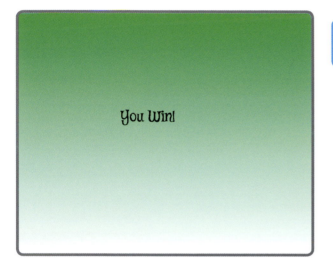

You Win!

 Use the text tool to type a winning message on your backdrop. (You can change the font using the drop-down menu at the bottom of your screen.)

STEP 3: Use the paintbrush tool to create a new backdrop. This will be your maze. First, click *Convert to vector** at the bottom right of your screen.

New backdrop:

paintbrush

*Vector mode makes it easy to fix small details as you go. You can click on a line in your maze and adjust it after it's been created. Just click the mouse icon, then click the line, and sizing dots will appear. (You can't do that in bitmap mode.) We'll talk more about vector mode (and bitmap mode) in the tools on page 79.

Font:
Gloria ▾

100%

Bitmap Mode
Convert to vector

maze   Name the backdrop *maze*.

 Use the line tool to draw your maze. (Hold down shift to draw straight lines.) Use any color except one that has already been used in your ball sprites. (Using one of the ball sprites' colors will cause confusion in the code when you use color sensing.)

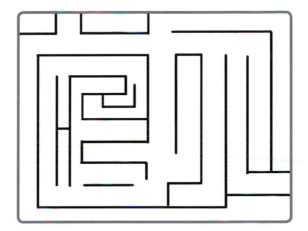

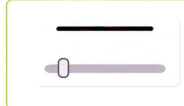 Adjust the line's thickness using the slide bar on the bottom left.

STEP 4: Duplicate the maze backdrop using the stamp tool. Add text on top of the duplicated backdrop saying, *You ran out of time!* or whatever message you'd like to appear on the game-over screen.

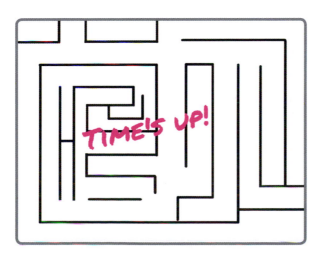

Time's Up!   When you're done, name the screen *Time's Up!*

 Use the text tool to create the message across the maze.

STEP 5: Add the below code onto the blue and yellow ball sprites.

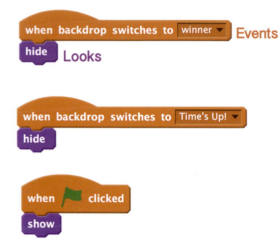

This tells them that when the background switches to either the *winner* or *Time's Up* screen they should hide. When the green flag is clicked at the start of the game, they should show.

STEP 6: Go to the Scripts tab (of any sprite), open **Data**, and click *Make a Variable*. A variable is a value that can change throughout the project. However, the value won't change unless it is coded to do so. Once you've created a new variable, name it *timer* and select *For all sprites*. (Now you'll be able to use this variable for all the sprites in your project.)

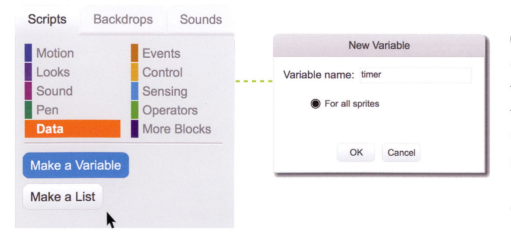

Once the variable has been created, you will have access to the code blocks necessary to change it as needed! You'll use these blocks later in the project. Make sure *For all sprites* is checked when you create your variable.

STEP 7: Arrange the balls and timer on the maze backdrop as shown:

Use the shrink tool to fit the balls inside the maze. Drag the timer variable to a spot on your screen that looks best for your maze.

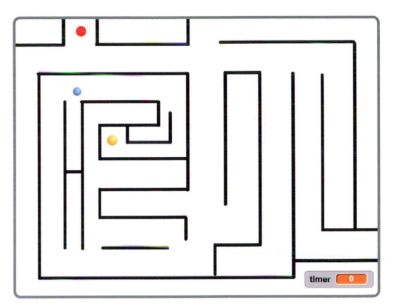

shrink tool

STEP 8: Add this code to the red ball sprite. These blocks will let you control the ball using the arrow keys.

when [up arrow ▾] key pressed   Events
change y by (10)   Motion

when [down arrow ▾] key pressed
change y by (-10)

when [right arrow ▾] key pressed
change x by (10)

when [left arrow ▾] key pressed
change x by (-10)

STEP 9: Add this additional code to the blue ball—or whichever ball is moving around the maze in hopes of keeping the main ball from succeeding.

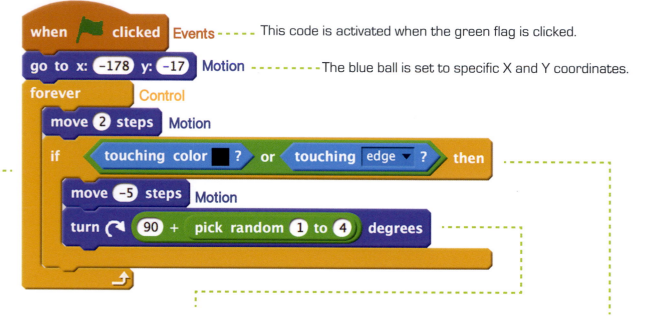

when [flag] clicked **Events** ----- This code is activated when the green flag is clicked.

go to x: -178 y: -17 **Motion** --------The blue ball is set to specific X and Y coordinates.

forever **Control**

move 2 steps **Motion**

if (touching color [ ] ? or touching edge ?) then

move -5 steps **Motion**

turn ↻ (90 + pick random 1 to 4) degrees

Put together two **Operators** blocks and a *turn* block from **Motion** to create this block.

Use the *or* block from **Operators** and two **Sensing** blocks to make this big block.

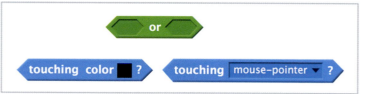

The coordinates in your project will differ from what you see here, because your maze will be different. Just place the ball where you'd like it to start within the maze, and the coordinates will automatically fill into the block.

The ball will then forever move two steps, with the condition that if it touches the edge of the screen or the color black—the maze color—then it will move -5 steps (away from the edge of the maze) and turn 90 degrees times either one, two, three, or four. This means the ball will move directly up, down, right, or left, and continue moving until the condition is met again. (The number 90 is used because 90 degrees is a right angle.)

STEP 10: Add this code to the background. It doesn't matter which background you choose; the code will be on all of them. (It's helpful to put *background changing* or *variable* codes onto the background so your sprites' Script sections doesn't get too cluttered.)

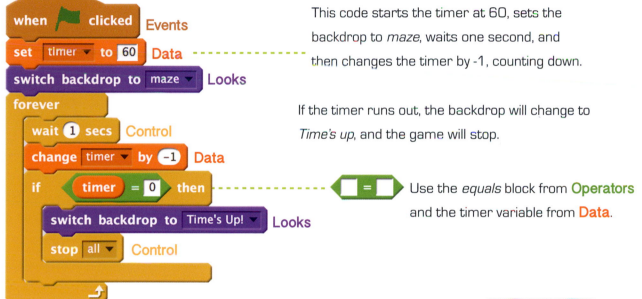

This code starts the timer at 60, sets the backdrop to *maze*, waits one second, and then changes the timer by -1, counting down.

If the timer runs out, the backdrop will change to *Time's up*, and the game will stop.

Use the *equals* block from **Operators** and the timer variable from **Data**.

New sound:

STEP 11: Click on the red ball sprite and select the Sounds tab. Open the Sound Library and select the *kick drum* and *fairydust* sounds. When you are finished, you should have *pop* (automatic), *kick drum,* and *fairydust* in the Sounds tab for the red ball sprite.

STEP 12: Add this code to the red ball sprite (or whichever ball is making its way through the maze) to finish coding this project.

This code is activated when the green flag is clicked.

Once it's clicked, the ball will show and go to a specific coordinate. (Just like with the blue ball, the coordinates in your project may be different from what's shown. Simply move the red ball to the starting point you'd like, and the coordinates will update. Once the numbers change, drag the *go to* block out.)

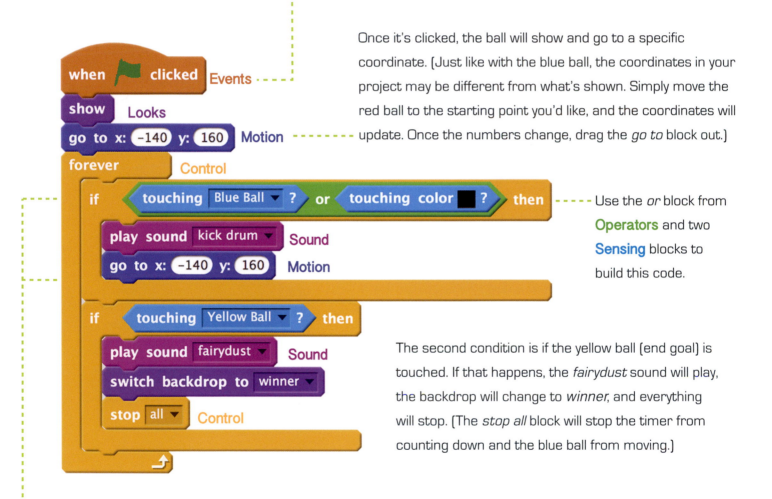

Use the *or* block from **Operators** and two **Sensing** blocks to build this code.

The second condition is if the yellow ball (end goal) is touched. If that happens, the *fairydust* sound will play, the backdrop will change to *winner*, and everything will stop. (The *stop all* block will stop the timer from counting down and the blue ball from moving.)

There are two conditions in this section of code. The first condition is if the blue ball or the maze are touched. If that happens, the *kick drum* sound will play and the red ball will go back to the start. (This condition will have the same coordinates as the *go to* block at the beginning of the code.)

Extras: If you'd like to customize your game, feel free to select different sounds. You could also add another moving ball as an obstacle in the maze. The code for the new ball would be the same as the blue ball code. You'd also need to add a *sensing* condition on the red ball sprite.

To make the game more challenging, play around with the amount of time you give players. The timer currently starts at 60, giving players a minute to navigate the maze. Try 50—or even 40!—and see how successful you can be.

TIP:

Coding is about making things your own, so don't be afraid to spice up this project or others. Try adding more code, if it doesn't work how you want it to, just throw that part away and try again. You can't break it!

Your maze game is finished! Use the arrow keys to move your balls around the maze, trying to get to the goal before the timer runs out. Use this link to view the finished game: https://scratch.mit.edu/projects/173332227/

HOW TO PLAY

Select the difficulty level at the start of the game—easy, medium or hard. Then move the paddle to bounce the ball, and avoid the ball getting to the bottom of the screen. Each time the ball gets past the paddle, you lose a life. Each time the ball bounces off the paddle, your score goes up by one. Try to get the highest score without losing all your lives!

LET'S GET STARTED!

STEP 1: Start a new project and name it *Ping Pong*. Delete Scratch Cat and select three button sprites from the Sprite Library. (You could also select one button sprite and duplicate it using the stamp tool.) Then use the Costumes tab to customize the buttons with whatever color you'd like. One by one, add the words *easy*, *medium*, and *hard* to the buttons using the text tool. You should now have a total of three sprites.

When you are done customizing the buttons, open the information tab for each sprite. Name the sprites *easy*, *medium*, and *hard*, depending on what text is written on each.

STEP 2: Select a ball sprite and a paddle sprite from the Sprite Library.

 In the Costumes tab, use the paint bucket tool to customize the color of the ball and paddle.

In the Sound Library for the ball sprite, add the *kick drum* sound effect.

kick drum

STEP 3: You need to create three separate costumes for your paddle—easy, medium, and hard. The easy paddle should be the largest, the medium paddle should be mid-size, and the hard paddle should be the smallest. (The smaller the paddle, the more challenging it is to hit the ball!)

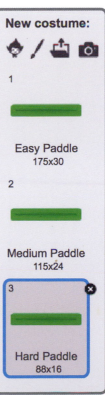

New costume:

1

Easy Paddle
175x30

2

Medium Paddle
115x24

3

Hard Paddle
88x16

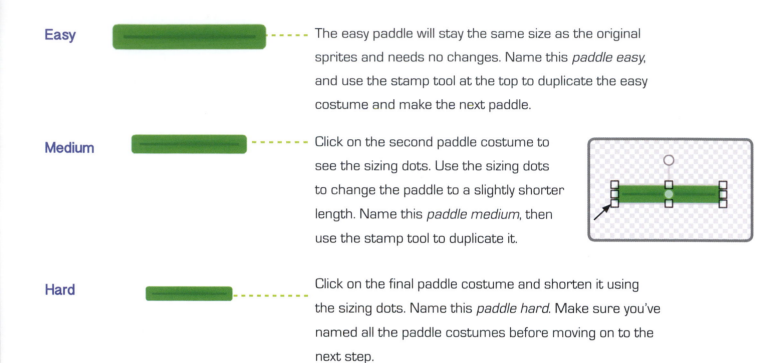

Easy — The easy paddle will stay the same size as the original sprites and needs no changes. Name this *paddle easy*, and use the stamp tool at the top to duplicate the easy costume and make the next paddle.

Medium — Click on the second paddle costume to see the sizing dots. Use the sizing dots to change the paddle to a slightly shorter length. Name this *paddle medium*, then use the stamp tool to duplicate it.

Hard — Click on the final paddle costume and shorten it using the sizing dots. Name this *paddle hard*. Make sure you've named all the paddle costumes before moving on to the next step.

STEP 4: Click on the Scripts tab (of any sprite) and then find **Data**. Create two new variables. Name them *score* and *lives*.

When you're finished, the **Data** section should look like this:

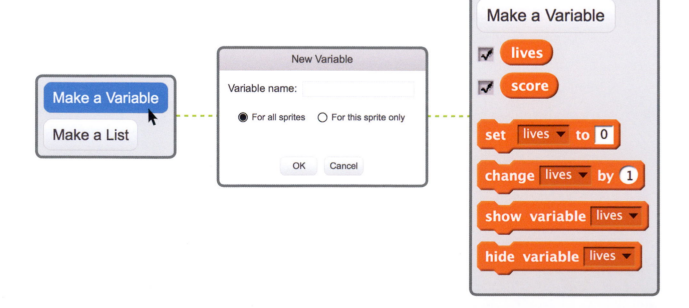

STEP 5: Use the paintbrush icon to make five new backdrops. Name them *level selector*, *easy*, *medium*, *hard*, and *game over*.

New backdrop:

paintbrush

 Use the paint bucket tool to fill each of your backdrops with two colors—black and the color of your choosing. Then use one of the two color-fill settings on the bottom left.

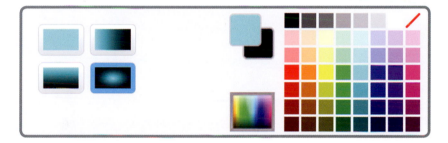

Level Selector

Easy

Medium

Hard

Game Over

 To type on the backgrounds, pick the color you want and use the text tool to type your message.

New backdrop:

1
Level Selector
480x360

2
Easy
480x360

3
Medium
480x360

4
Hard
480x360

5
Game Over
480x360

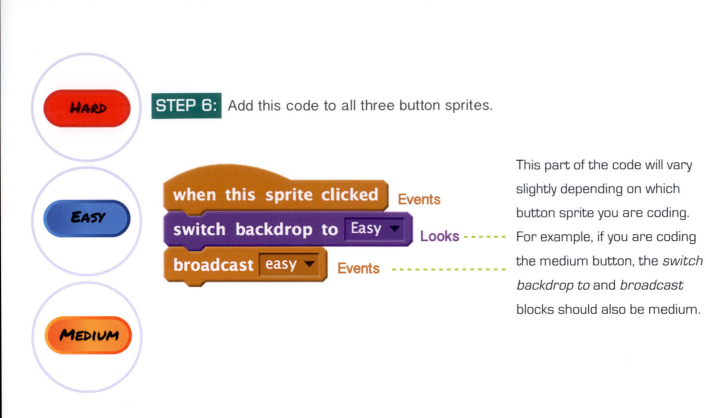

STEP 6: Add this code to all three button sprites.

This part of the code will vary slightly depending on which button sprite you are coding. For example, if you are coding the medium button, the *switch backdrop to* and *broadcast* blocks should also be medium.

To make the correct broadcasts, you will need to create three new messages in the broadcast block: *easy*, *medium*, and *hard*. This part of the code hides the button sprites on all backdrops except for the *level-selector* backdrop.

STEP 7: Add this code to your ball and paddle sprites. This hides the ball and paddle on the *level-selector* and *game-over* screens.

STEP 8: Add this code to the backdrop. This will reset the *score* and *lives* variables at the start of each game and switch the backdrop to *level selector*. It also tells the backdrop to change to *game over* and to stop if the number of lives reaches zero.

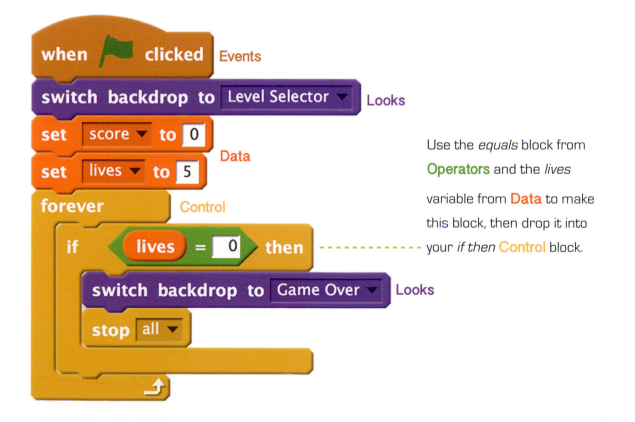

Use the *equals* block from **Operators** and the *lives* variable from **Data** to make this block, then drop it into your *if then* **Control** block.

WHEN IS IT HELPFUL TO CREATE YOUR OWN BLOCK?

The **More Blocks** category in the Scripts tab is helpful when you need to use a big piece of code repeatedly in a set of commands. In this case, we need the paddle to move, regardless of which broadcast (easy, medium, or hard) it receives.

Instead of coding the entire movement under each start command, we'll create a *paddle moves* block to simplify things. First, click on the **More Blocks** category under the Scripts tab. Then click *make a block*. Name the block *paddle move*. Add the below code to beneath *define paddle move* block.

Once you've defined what the *paddle move* block is, you can click on **More Blocks** again. Now you'll see the *paddle move* block here. Drag it into your code blocks as shown.

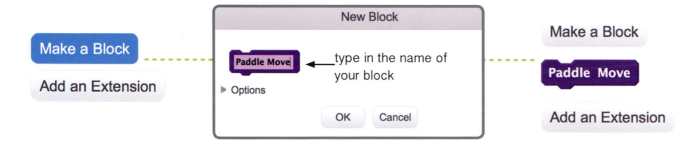

STEP 9: Add the code on this page to your paddle sprite. The *paddle move* code works by combining a *set X* block from **Motion** with a *mouse X* block from **Sensing**. Together they, along with the forever loop, allow the X (side to side) motion of the paddle to be the same as the X motion of the mouse. Therefore the paddle is controlled with the motion of the mouse.

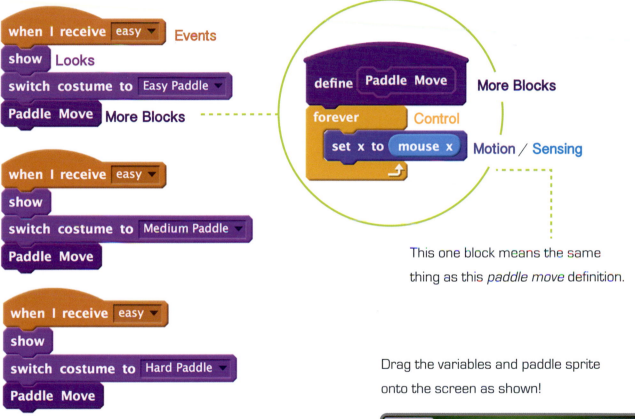

when I receive easy ▼ — Events
show — Looks
switch costume to Easy Paddle ▼
Paddle Move — More Blocks

define Paddle Move — More Blocks
forever — Control
set x to mouse x — Motion / Sensing

This one block means the same thing as this *paddle move* definition.

when I receive easy ▼
show
switch costume to Medium Paddle ▼
Paddle Move

when I receive easy ▼
show
switch costume to Hard Paddle ▼
Paddle Move

Drag the variables and paddle sprite onto the screen as shown!

TIP:
Go back through previous projects and figure out how to control the paddle with the left and right arrow keys! You can find lots of help in the Save Scratch Cat game on page 36.

Score 0   Lives 5

STEP 10: You need to create and define two new blocks here—*paddle bounce* and *check lives*—just like we did for *paddle move* in step 9. Then add the code on the next page to the ball sprite to complete this project!

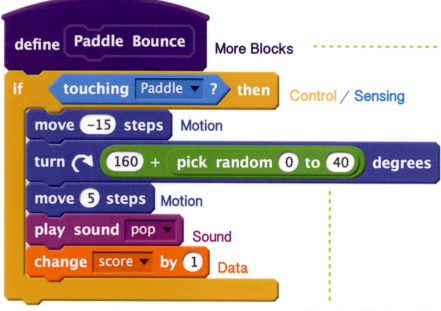

Create the *paddle bounce* block by clicking **More Blocks**, then clicking *Make a Block*. Name the block *paddle bounce*. Then add this code (everything from the **Control** block on) to the new block. When you place this block into your larger code block, it will cause the ball to move back, turn anywhere from 160 to 200 degrees, and turn away from the paddle at a random position. Then the sound *pop* will play and the score variable will change by one. This will all happen when the ball touches the paddle sprite.

Use *plus* block and the *pick random* block from **Operators** to make this block. Then drop it into the *turn___degrees* block from **Motion**.

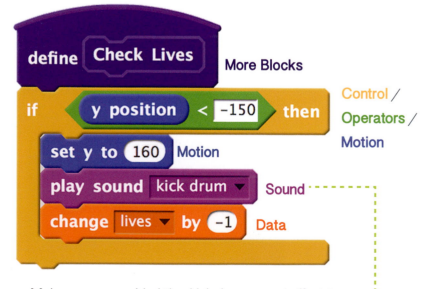

Create the *check lives* block by clicking on **More Blocks**, then clicking *Make a Block*. Name the block *check lives*. Then add this code (everything from the **Control** block on) to the new block. This code checks if the ball has fallen too far down the screen. If the ball's *Y* position (up and down) is less than -150 that means it has gone below the paddle sprite and was missed. The ball must then go back to the top of the screen (*set Y to 160*), the *kick drum* sound will play, and then the *lives* variable will change by -1.

Make sure you added the *kick drum* sound effect to the ball sprite in step 2 so you can select it here.

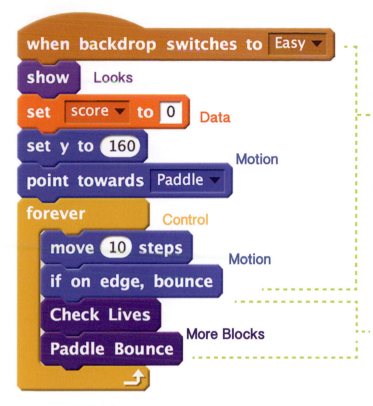

When the backdrops switch to *easy*, *medium*, or *hard*, the ball sprite needs to show up and the score needs to reset to zero. The ball must start at the top of the screen (*set Y to 160*) and point toward the paddle. Then the ball will forever move 10, 12, or 15 steps, depending on the level of difficulty. (Change these numbers as you'd like.) If the ball touches the edge, it will bounce.

The last part of the code is the *check lives* and *paddle bounce* blocks. Since you already created the long explanation for the blocks, you can now use the short block at the end of the code that you see here. These blocks will allow the ball to bounce off the paddle and change either the *score* or *lives* variable if the condition is met.

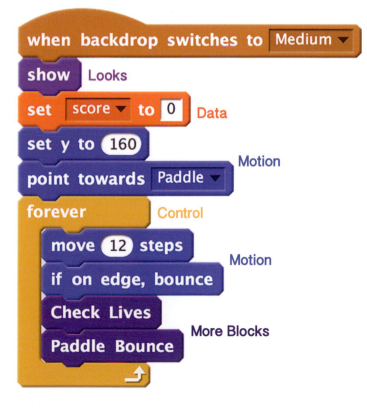

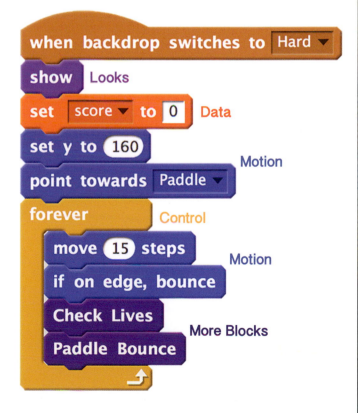

See the finished game here: https://scratch.mit.edu/projects/116622727/

ANIMATION
AND
PRESENTATION

One of the best parts about coding with Scratch is your ability to create your own backdrops and sprites. There are endless possibilities! If you're having trouble finding the perfect sprite or background for your project, stop hunting for it and just make it!

BITMAP MODE VS. VECTOR MODE

There are two different modes you can use for creating your own backgrounds and sprites—**bitmap** or **vector**.

Convert to bitmap

Bitmap mode makes it easy to fill in simple backgrounds and shapes. If you need to create a quick shape or background, use the design tools in this mode. (But keep in mind that if you make a shape and need to resize it later, bitmap mode won't allow it.)

Convert to vector

Vector mode has many of the same tools but is more flexible. It lets you reshape or resize shapes you've made. You can also create another shape and then go back to a previous one to move it. Vector is more useful for detailed backgrounds and sprites.

Bitmap design tools appear on
the left of the backdrop screen.

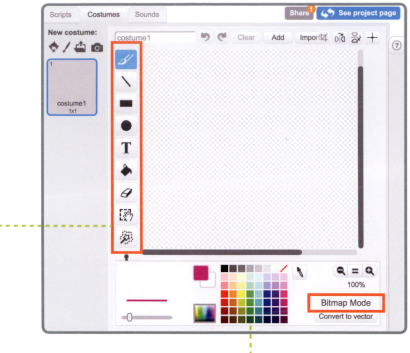

Colors will always show on the bottom
of your creation screen.

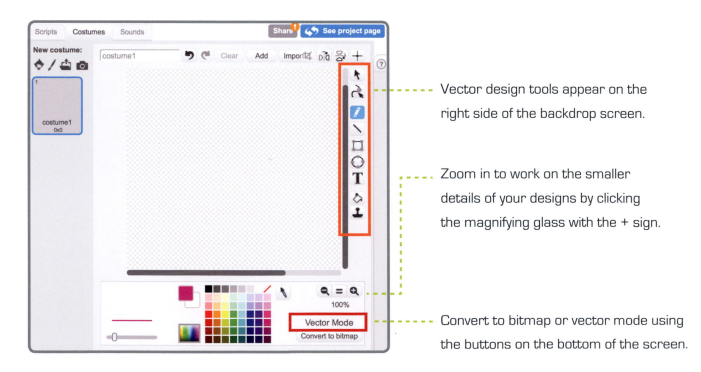

Vector design tools appear on the
right side of the backdrop screen.

Zoom in to work on the smaller
details of your designs by clicking
the magnifying glass with the + sign.

Convert to bitmap or vector mode using
the buttons on the bottom of the screen.

For details on what each tool does, keep reading!

BITMAP MODE TOOLS:

paintbrush—Use the paintbrush tool to draw freehand. Click and drag the mouse around to paint. Change the thickness of the paintbrush using the width slider on the bottom left of the screen.

line—Use this tool to draw lines. Click and drag the mouse until the line is your desired length. To create a perfectly straight line, press and hold shift while drawing.

rectangle—Click the rectangle icon, then drag the mouse diagonally to create a rectangle. (Once you've selected this tool, you can choose either a hollow or filled-in rectangle at the bottom of the screen.) To make a perfect square, press and hold shift while creating the shape.

circle—Click the circle icon, then drag the mouse diagonally to create a circle. (Once you've selected this tool, you can select either a hollow or filled-in circle at the bottom of the screen.) To make a perfect circle, press and hold shift while creating the shape.

text—Select the T icon to add text to your design. Click inside the box until you see a cursor, then select the color and font you'd like at the bottom of the screen. To make the text larger, click out of the text box, then stretch the text using the sizing dots.

paint bucket—Use this tool to fill in the background or a shape with a certain color. If you're filling in a shape, be sure that there are no gaps in the drawing, otherwise the paint will leak out and fill the entire page! (You may need to zoom in to see if there are any gaps—sometimes they're hard to spot!)

eraser—Use this tool to remove things from your project. Just click and drag the mouse across the object you want to remove. To change the size of the eraser, use the scroll bar on the bottom of the screen.

 grabber—Use the grabber to delete, move, or stretch something. Just drag a box around the item and get to work!

 magic wand—Use the magic wand to remove backgrounds on any images you've uploaded.

stamp—Use the stamp to duplicate something you've made.

Line width:

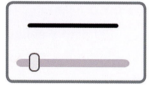

Filled-in or hollow shape:

Eraser size:

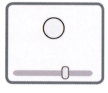

VECTOR MODE:

 mouse pointer—Use the pointer to reselect a shape after you've created it. Once you select the shape, you can resize, move, or delete it.

 reshape—The reshape tool lets you make changes to a circle or square you've already created. For details on how to use this tool, turn the page and check out the instructions on page 85.

 pencil—Use this tool to draw freehand. Change the thickness of the line using the scrollbar at the bottom of the screen.

 line—Use this tool to draw lines in your project. Click and drag the mouse until the line is your desired length. To create a perfectly straight line, press and hold shift while creating drawing.

 square—Click the square icon, then drag the mouse diagonally to create a square. (Once you've selected this tool, you can choose either a hollow or filled-in square at the bottom of the screen.) To make a perfect square, press and hold shift while creating the shape.

 circle—Click the circle icon, then drag the mouse diagonally to create a circle. (Once you've selected this tool, you can choose either a hollow or filled-in circle at the bottom of the screen.) To make a perfect circle, press and hold shift while creating the shape.

 text—Select the T icon to add a text box to your design. Click inside the box until you see a cursor, then select the color and font you'd like at the bottom of the screen. To make the text larger, click out of the text box, then stretch the text using the sizing dots.

paint bucket—Use the paint bucket to color in shapes you've created. (Keep in mind the paint bucket won't fill in the entire background unless you make a big square to fill it. It won't fill in images you've drawn unless it is a closed shape.)

 **stamp**—Use the stamp to duplicate different shapes. This is helpful when you want two shapes to be identical, like a pair of eyes!

up arrow/down arrow—These tools move objects forward or behind other shapes in a drawing. They will appear when you have more than one image in the creation space. The up arrow brings an object forward a layer, and the down arrow moves something back a layer. (For example, if you made a large shape and want it behind a smaller shape, click the down arrow to send it back a layer so the smaller shape is on top.)

 group—Use this tool when you have used multiple shapes to create something and you'd like them all to move as one object. Use the mouse pointer to draw a box around the shapes, then click this icon to group them together.

ungroup—Use this tool to separate objects or shapes that are grouped together.

USING THE RESHAPE TOOL

To use the reshape tool, be sure that you made your circle or square in vector mode. (If you created it in bitmap, you won't be able to reshape it.)

Create a shape.

Click the reshape icon, and then click on the shape you made. Reshape dots will appear.

Push or pull the reshape dots until you have your desired shape.

MAKING AN EYEBALL:

An eye may seem like a basic shape, but creating one involves a few different tools. To make an eyeball, click on the paintbrush in the sprite toolbar to draw your own sprite.

paintbrush

Click *Convert to vector* at the bottom right of the screen.

Use the circle tool to draw and layer three circles: one large white circle, one medium black circle, and one small white circle. Make sure all three are filled in, and layer them like this:

 Check that you are using vector mode so you can move the circles around as needed!

 When you finish drawing the eye, click on the mouse pointer and draw a box around it.

 Click the group icon so you can move, shrink, or grow all three circles as one eye.

Let's use some more shapes to create this cute little guy!

Create a red circle and place the eye on top of it.

Draw a small smile using the black pencil. (You can increase the thickness of the line using the sliding toolbar at the bottom left.)

Draw a big red oval for the body. Then using the circle tool, create a thin oval for the right arm. Use the top circle to rotate the oval slightly, then drag it into position on the body.

Using the duplicate tool, make an identical arm for the other side. Click the *flip image* icon at the top right to rotate the arm in the correct direction. Drag it to the opposite side of the body.

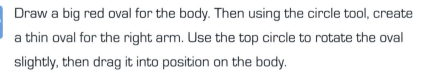

TIP:

Don't be afraid to use the undo and redo arrows if you make a mistake! They can be very helpful. As you work through the projects to come, you'll be creating lots of sprites and backdrops. Refer to this page for help if you ever get lost.

THE GOAL:

Make a pen that can be moved around the screen to create a drawing. Pick from either a pencil or fun rainbow pen!

LET'S GET STARTED!

STEP 1: Start a new project and delete Scratch Cat. Then select three button sprites from the Sprite Library. (You can also choose one button sprite and use the stamp tool to duplicate it twice.) Drag the sprites so they are stacked along the right side of your background. (You will be drawing all over the background, so you don't want them to get in the way of your art!)

scissors   Sprite Library   Button3   Button2   Button4

STEP 2: Open the Sprite Library again and select the sprite you'd like to use as the drawing tool in your project. (For this project, we're using the pencil sprite.)

TIP:
Remember that sprites are grouped by category and sorted alphabetically in the Sprite Library.

STEP 3: Open the Costumes tab on each of the button sprites to customize it. Use the paint bucket to fill in each button using a different color. Use the text tool to create a text box inside each button.

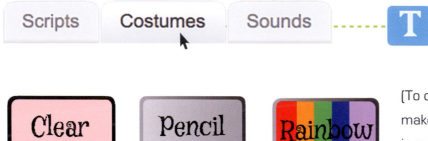

(To create the rainbow effect, make multiple filled-in rectangles in rainbow colors and put them inside the button. Then add the text on top!)

STEP 4: Open each sprite's information tab by clicking the small blue *i* and name the buttons *clear*, *rainbow*, and *pencil*. Name your drawing tool (in this case, the pencil) *magic pen*.

TIP:
If the paint bucket isn't successfully filling in the whole background, make sure you're in bitmap mode at the bottom right of your screen.

STEP 5: Click on the paintbrush icon to create a new backdrop. Use the paint bucket to fill in the background with a solid color and use the text tool to type the words *magic pen*. (Keep it simple—the background is designed to be drawn on when the project is completed.)

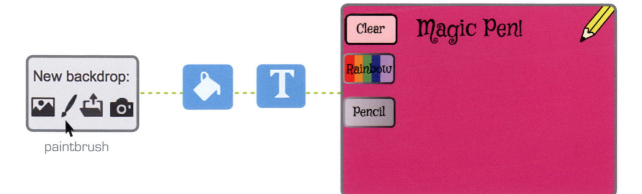

paintbrush

STEP 6: Add this code to the backdrop under the Scripts tab.

when 🚩 clicked **Events** --------- This code will activate when the green flag is clicked.

clear graphic effects **Looks**

forever **Control**

change color ▼ effect by (pick random 1 to 200) **Looks / Operators**

wait 0.5 secs **Control**

The graphic effects will clear, and the background will change to a random color. It will wait 0.5 seconds and continue forever.

If you want the background to change at a different pace, just increase or decrease the wait time!

STEP 7: Add this code to your three button sprites.

when this sprite clicked
broadcast clear ▼

when this sprite clicked
broadcast rainbow ▼

when this sprite clicked
broadcast Pencil ▼

Use one code block per button. You'll need to create a new broadcast in the drop-down menu for each. (A broadcast is like sending a message. You'll create the broadcast to be sent, and later you'll code other sprites to activate a certain code when the broadcast has been received.) Name the broadcast to match your button.

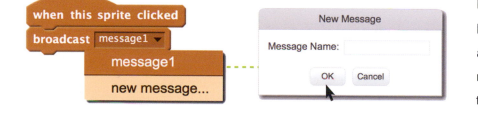

Use the broadcast block in **Events** and create a new message to make these blocks.

STEP 8: Add the following code blocks to the Scripts tab of your magic pen sprite.

When the *clear* message is received from the clear button, all graphic effects (drawing) will clear.

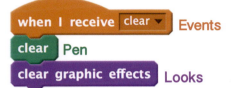

When the space bar is pressed, all code will stop. The pen won't follow the mouse pointer anymore.

When the pencil broadcast is received, the pen will change its size to a small pencil-like size and set its color to purple. Then it will forever follow the mouse and have the pen down so it can draw.

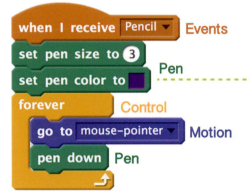

When the rainbow broadcast is received, the pen will change its size to 1 so it starts tiny. Then it will go to the mouse pointer. The pen will go down and the pen color and size will continue to forever change, causing the rainbow color to show and pen size to gradually increase*.

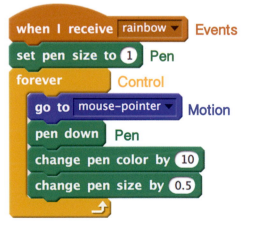

*If you don't want the pen to grow larger and would prefer just the rainbow ink, just take out the *change pen size by* block.

WHAT IS THE PEN CATEGORY IN SCRIPTS?

The *pen down* code block lets sprites draw lines wherever they move. Think about it as though every sprite has a pen hidden inside. You can code the pen to appear and tell it when to disappear into the sprite again so it will stop making a line when it moves. You can also code the color and size of the pen. Cool, right?

TIP:

Remember, to select the color for the *set pen color to* block, click inside the square. A small white finger cursor will appear. When the cursor appears, move it over to the color you'd like to select and click on it.

 You're all set! View your project in full-screen mode to start drawing. Select the color of your choice, then move your mouse to create your own work of art! Click the space bar to stop drawing and the clear button to erase. See the finished project here: https://scratch.mit.edu/projects/125092281/

Bouncing Gummy Bears

THE PROJECT:

Create a gummy bear that will bounce when you click on it. You'll make several different costumes and code the bear to switch through them to make it look like it's moving.

LET'S GET STARTED!

STEP 1: Open a new project screen and delete Scratch Cat. You won't need him here. Then use paintbrush in the drawing tools to draw a big gummy bear sprite. Make sure to use the drawing tools in **vector mode** since you'll need to adjust the gummy bear's size.

scissors   paintbrush

 Create the gummy bear's head using the filled-in circle tool. Use the same tool to draw the ears, reshaping them slightly. (Save time by duplicating the first ear to make the second. Use the *flip left-right* icon, like you did on page 86, to flip the arn.) Continue using the circle tool to draw the body, which will be more of an oval. Draw the paws, this time using the outlined circle. Choose a slightly darker red for the outline so the paws are visible. Then use the paint bucket tool to fill in the paws so they match the body and ears.

 Duplicate the paw using the stamp tool until you have four paws. Arrange them on the bear's body.

Using the same darker red, select the pencil tool and add the mouth, nose, and ear details. Then use the circle tool to draw a white circle for the eyes. (You'll need to reshape it slightly to match what you see here.) Add a large black circle and smaller white circle to the center of the eye.

> **TIP:**
> It will help to group all the pieces of the eye together and duplicate it so the second eye is identical to the first!

STEP 2: To make it look like the gummy bear is being squished, you'll need to create multiple costumes for your sprite. Each costume will have a very slight change. To start, duplicate the gummy bear's first costume so you have an exact copy. (This new costume will automatically be named *costume2*.)

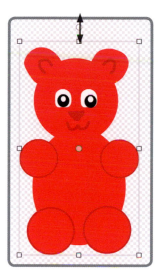

Working in *costume2*, use the pointer tool to draw a box around the entire bear and shrink him just a little. Then click on just the head and reshape it to look slightly squished. The difference should be so small it is hardly noticeable! Duplicate *costume2* to create *costume3*.

TIP:

If you accidentally select other parts of the bear's body, don't worry! Just click on the drawing screen so the box disappears and try again until you have successfully grabbed just the eyes!

Working in *costume3*, drag a box around the whole bear and shrink him again. Then drag a box around just the eyes. Shrink them a bit using the sizing dots that appear. (Make sure you start your box in the drawing area—outside the bear's body—so you don't move anything else.) Each time you duplicate the costume, the part you squish down will be farther down the bear's body, just like if you squished it with your finger. Duplicate *costume3* to make *costume4*.

Working in *costume4*, drag a box around the whole bear again and shrink him. Then shrink just his top paws!

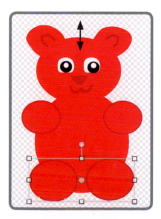

Duplicate *costume4* to create *costume5*.

Working in *costume5*, draw a box around the entire bear and shrink him slightly. Then do the same to just the bottom paws.

STEP 3: You should now have five costumes total. So far the costumes have squished the bear down little by little. Now it's time to start building him back up. You don't need to make any further changes to the bear. You will now duplicate the costumes in reverse order.

Duplicate *costume4* again to create *costume6*. (Use *costume4* because it is just slightly taller than *costume5*.)

Duplicate *costume3* to create *costume7*.

Finally, duplicate *costume2* to make *costume8*.

STEP 4: Create a new backdrop and use the paint bucket to fill it in with any color and effect you like.

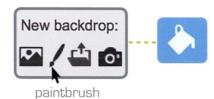

paintbrush

New costume:

1 costume1
168x300

2 costume2
168x297

3 costume3
168x279

4 costume4
168x265

5 costume5
168x253

6 costume6
174x272

7 costume7
174x286

8 costume8
174x305

STEP 5: Add this code to the gummy bear sprite's Scripts tab. Then open the sprite's information and name it *red gummy bear*.

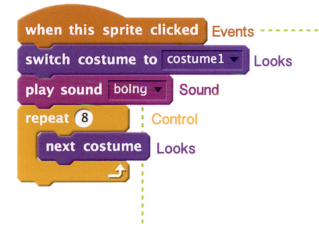

This code will activate when the gummy bear sprite is clicked. The costume will start on *costume1*, then it will play the sound *boing* and repeat through the costumes eight times, ending at the eighth costume.

You'll need to go into the Sound Library and add the *boing* sound effect before you can select it in the drop-down menu of the **Sound** block.

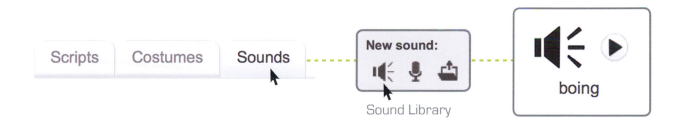

STEP 6: To make your project more complex, add another bear. Use the stamp tool to duplicate the *red gummy bear* sprite; name the new sprite *green gummy bear*. Then open the Costumes tab and use the paint bucket to fill in the new gummy bear so it's all green. Use a darker green for any details, like the mouth and ears.

shrink tool

Use the shrink tool to shrink down *green gummy bear* sprite if you want it to be smaller. Now you'll have two bouncing gummy bears! All lined up, your costumes should look like this—there will be eight total:

You're finished! Click on the *See project page* button at the top right to view your finished project. Click on your gummy bear to watch him shrink and grow! See the finished project here: https://scratch.mit.edu/projects/174282643/

THE PROJECT:

Create a parrot that will soar through the air by flapping its wings!

LET'S GET STARTED!

STEP 1: Open a new project and name it. Delete Scratch Cat, then use the paintbrush to create a new sprite. (Be sure to switch to **vector mode** before drawing the parrot. You'll need to be able to change it later.)

scissors   paintbrush

 Use the circle tool to draw the parrot's body. Select the filled-in circle option at the bottom left of the screen and choose the body color. (We used red.) Make the body more of an oval shape. Then use the same tool to create the parrot's wings. You'll need to draw multiple oval shapes—one big oval for the wing and lots of small ovals for the feathers. We've used the colors red, white, and blue. (Use the stamp tool in your vector toolbar to duplicate the smaller circles for the feathers and rotate them as needed.)

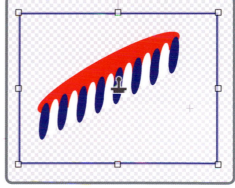

 When you have one wing created, draw a box around it and use the grouping tool to group all the pieces together. Then you can easily duplicate the wing. Flip it using the *flip image* tool at the top. You should now have two identical wings.

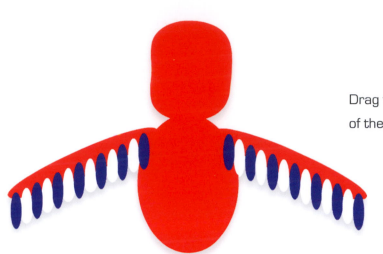

Drag the wings onto opposite sides of the parrot's body.

 To create the parrot's face, use the circle tool to draw an oval. Make it the same color as the parrot's body. Then use a different color to draw a smaller circle. Place it on top of the larger circle.

To make the eye, draw a white circle outlined in black. Reshape it slightly to match what you see here, then add the black circle and smaller white circle to the inside. Draw a box around the eye and then group all the pieces together before dragging it into position.

Use the circle tool to draw an oval for the beak, then reshape it to be more beaklike. Finally, use the pencil tool to draw the parrot's claws. (Your beak and claws should be the same color.)

STEP 2: To make it look like the parrot is flying through the sky, you'll need to create multiple costumes. The wings will be in a slightly different position in each costume. (If you didn't group the pieces of the wings together when you made the sprite, do that now.) Start off by duplicating the first parrot costume using the stamp tool. This will create *costume2*.

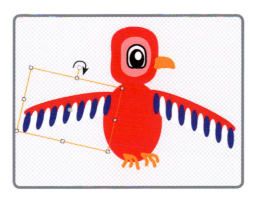

Working in *costume2*, use the mouse pointer tool and click on the wing to select it. Then use the small dot on the top to rotate the wing up slightly. Do the same thing on the other wing. The difference will hardly be noticeable at first!

Continue duplicating the parrot costume until you have 10 costumes. Working through each costume (in order) rotate the wings slightly more than in the previous costume. By *costume10*, the wings will be pointing up.

STEP 3: Use the paintbrush in the backdrop tools to create a new backdrop. Then use the tools in your toolbar to draw a backdrop that looks like the sky. (It's OK to draw your backdrop in bitmap mode since you won't be changing it.) Don't forget to add clouds and a sun!

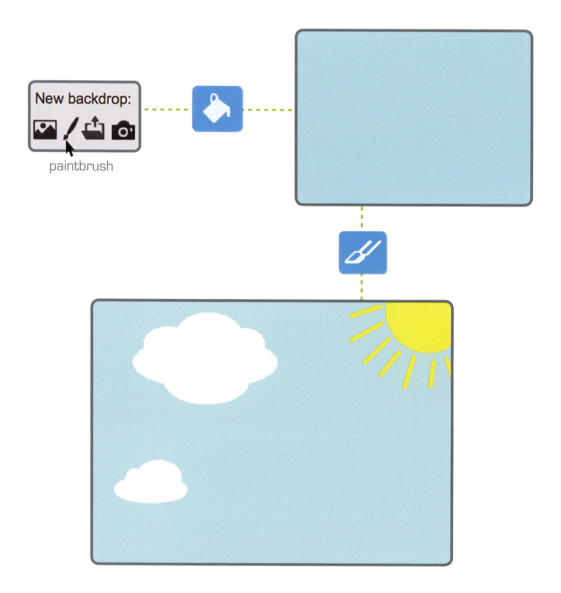

STEP 4: Add the below code blocks to your parrot sprite. This code will tell the parrot to move using the arrow keys and switch through its costumes to make it look like the wings are flapping.

The X and Y in the **Motion** block refers to the X and Y axes of a coordinate plane. The X axis runs horizontally (left and right). The Y axis runs vertically (up and down). If you have a positive Y coordinate it will be in the upper half of the plane. A negative Y coordinate will be found on the lower half. A positive X coordinate will be found on the right side. A negative X coordinate will be found on the left side.

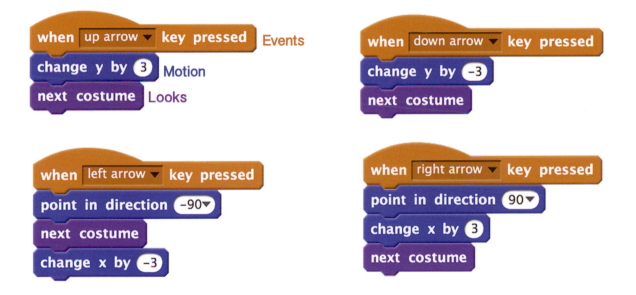

You're finished! View your project in full-screen mode, and use the arrow keys to watch your parrot fly around the page. See the finished project here: https://scratch.mit.edu/projects/174286343/

ALL About You Presentation

THE PROJECT:

Click the different buttons to share information about yourself in a fun new way!

LET'S GET STARTED!

STEP 1: Open a new project and create a new backdrop. (Go ahead and delete Scratch Cat—we won't need him for this presentation.) This will be your start screen. Use the paint bucket and text box tools to edit the background, filling it in with a solid color and adding text to the background. Name it *All About Me*.

scissors

paintbrush

ALL ABOUT ME!

Think about what types of things you want to share about yourself. We've used favorite color, animal, candy, food, sport, and season. If you want to pick more favorites or replace an example with something else, go for it! The awesome part about coding is that you can personalize everything. This project is all about YOU, so change the categories to fit your personality.

STEP 2: Add six button sprites from the Sprite Library. (You can also add one button sprite and use the stamp tool to duplicate it five times.) Once you have your button sprites, open the Costumes tab for each and customize it with a category. (We've used candy, season, food, color, sport, and animal.)

Sprite Library

 Use the paint bucket and text tool to customize the button sprites. (Click the 🛈 to open the sprite's information box and name each one.)

You can arrange your buttons on your start screen however you'd like!

CANDY FOOD ANIMAL

SEASON COLOR SPORTS

STEP 3: Use the paintbrush icon in your backdrop toolbar to make unique backdrops for each of your six buttons. Add your own answer for each category you created. You will create new backdrops, one per button, until you have a total of seven, including your *All About Me* screen! Be sure to name each background to match the button it goes with. (Example: The pizza background should be labeled *food* to match your *food* button.)

paintbrush

STEP 4: Add the below code block to all your button sprites. (Look at page 119 for a quick tip on how to code from one sprite to another.)

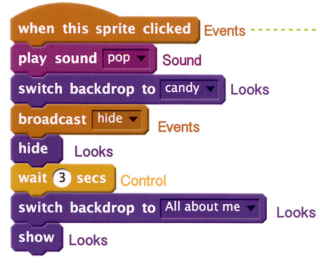

This code is activated when the button sprite is clicked. When the button is clicked, the *pop* sound will play and the background will switch. Then a hide broadcast will be sent to all the button sprites, three seconds will pass, and the background will switch back to the *All About Me* backdrop.

Don't forget to update the backdrop name in the *switch backdrop to* **Looks** block so it matches the button sprite you're coding. (For example, the above code block belongs on the candy button sprite.) You'll also need to create a new broadcast using the drop-down menu in the **Events** block. This broadcast won't change from sprite to sprite. Once it has been created, it will stay the same on all.

When the hide broadcast is received, the button sprites hide, wait for 3 seconds, and show back up.

To add even more to this project, spice up the backgrounds by drawing different pictures on them, like the cotton candy and pizza in step 3. You could even add special sounds for each button and code them to play when the backgrounds switch. Play around with it and have fun creating a project that's all about YOU! See the finished project here: https://scratch.mit.edu/projects/174293179/

THE PROJECT:

Click the space bar to move through this how-to project on making yummy spaghetti. Click on the images below each step to see them move.

LET'S GET STARTED!

STEP 1: Start a new project, delete Scratch Cat, and use the paintbrush icon to create your own intro screen. On this backdrop, describe what your tutorial will be. (Ours is *How to Make Spaghetti*.) At the bottom of the screen, add a note that says *click the space bar to begin.* When you're finished, name this backdrop *Start Screen*.

scissors

New backdrop:

paintbrush

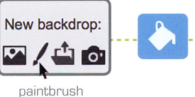

Use the paint bucket and text tools to edit your background, adding the color and text.

Feel free to draw some extra pictures to this backdrop; it can be as simple or crazy as you'd like!

To create this two-color effect, select two colors when filling in the paint bucket. Then select the fill type you'd like in the bottom left corner. Use the drop-down menu on the bottom left to change the font if you'd like.

How to Make Spaghetti

CLICK THE SPACE BAR TO BEGIN.

STEP 2: Add this code to the Scripts tab of your backdrop. When the green flag is clicked, the backdrop will switch to your start screen. When space bar is pressed, it will go to next backdrop.

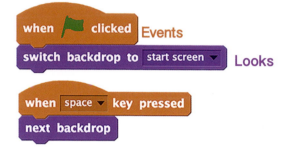

STEP 3: Use the paintbrush in the backdrop toolbar to make new backdrops for the steps of your tutorial. Keep it to just two steps per page—you'll need to leave room for the animated sprites you'll add later. Create your backdrop(s) in vector mode so you can change the text from backdrop to backdrop.

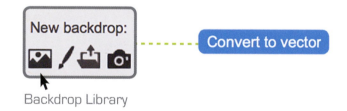

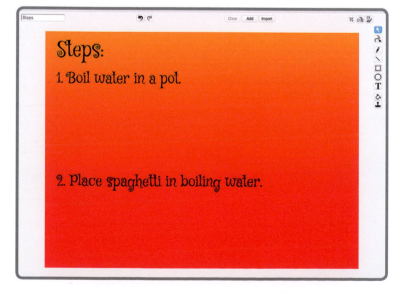

Name the first screen *Steps*. Then use the stamp tool at the top of the screen to duplicate this backdrop. Change the steps/instructions on the background. This backdrop will automatically be named *Steps2*. Duplicate and change the steps again for *Steps3**.

* If your tutorial requires more steps than this example, keep going! You can have as many pages as you need. Just be sure to name each step so you can keep them straight later.

STEP 4: Use the paintbrush icon to create the sprites for your steps. The first step in making spaghetti is to boil a pot of water. You'll need a pot sprite! Use vector mode so you can easily make changes to the sprite later.

paintbrush

Start with a simple pot. Use the circle tool to draw a circle outlined in gray and filled in with blue (for the water). Then draw a curved square for the bottom and a rectangle for the handle. (You may need to rotate the rectangle slightly, or use the *forward a layer/back a layer* tools to layer things correctly.) Name the finished sprite *pot*.

STEP 5: Duplicate the pot costume and add flames. Name this costume *flame 1*.

Duplicate the *flame 1* costume and change the flames a bit. Add small gray dots that look like bubbles to the water. (These represent the water boiling.) This costume will automatically be named *flame 2*.

Duplicate *flame 2*; move the bubbles around a bit and adjust the flame slightly to create *flame 3*. Repeat this process once more to create *flame 4*.

STEP 6: Add the code below onto the pot sprite.

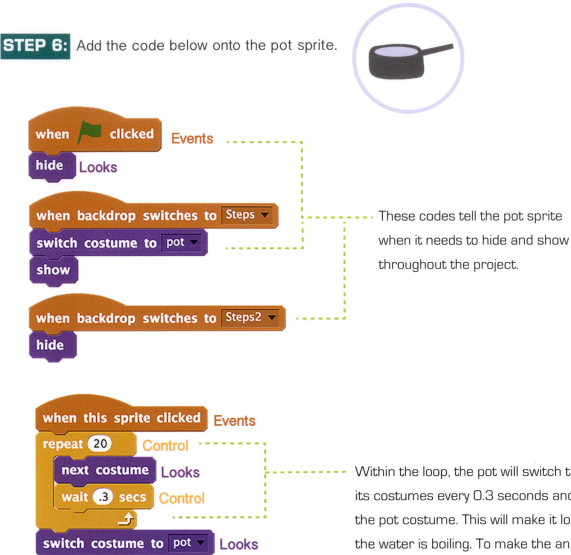

when ⚑ clicked — Events
hide — Looks

when backdrop switches to Steps ▼
switch costume to pot ▼
show

These codes tell the pot sprite when it needs to hide and show throughout the project.

when backdrop switches to Steps2 ▼
hide

when this sprite clicked — Events
repeat 20 — Control
  next costume — Looks
  wait .3 secs — Control
switch costume to pot ▼ — Looks

Within the loop, the pot will switch through its costumes every 0.3 seconds and end on the pot costume. This will make it look like the water is boiling. To make the animation last longer, increase the number of times the code repeats within the loop.

STEP 7: Use the paintbrush icon in the sprite toolbar to draw a spaghetti sprite. Use the drawing tools to make long, straight lines to look like uncooked spaghetti. When you're finished, open the sprite's information and name it *raw spaghetti*.

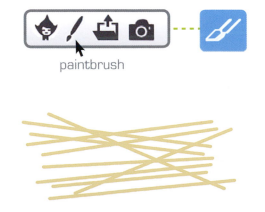

paintbrush

STEP 8: Add the code below to the *raw spaghetti* sprite.

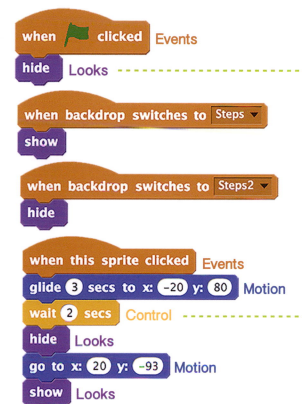

These blocks tell the *raw spaghetti* sprite to hide when the green flag is clicked and then to show or hide when the backdrop switches to different steps.

This code will activate when the sprite is clicked. It will then slowly glide up to where the pot sprite is. (To figure out the exact coordinates, drag the *raw spaghetti* sprite to the *pot* sprite on the screen. The code block coordinates will automatically update.) The *raw spaghetti* sprite will then wait two seconds, hide, and go back to its original spot. (For the X and Y coordinates here, drag the spaghetti back and the *go to* block will update.)

STEP 9: Arrange your sprites on the *Steps* backdrop to match the image below.

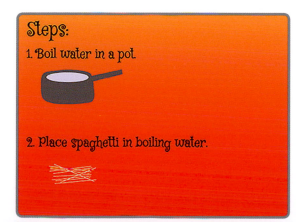

STEP 10: Use the paintbrush icon in the sprite toolbar to draw a clock sprite. Use the drawing tools in vector mode.

paintbrush

Convert to vector

Use the circle tool to create a circle outlined in black and filled in white. Then add a circle to the middle and draw two lines coming out for the minute and hour hands. Use the pencil tool to make the notches for the hours.

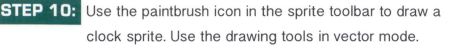

When you finish the first costume, duplicate it and change the minute hand slightly. Keep duplicating and rotating the minute hand until you have a total of four costumes. (They will automatically name themselves *costume1*, *costume2*, *costume3*, and *costume4*.)

STEP 11: Click on the paintbrush icon and use the vector drawing tools to create a new sprite that looks like plain cooked spaghetti on a plate.

paintbrush

Convert to vector

To make the plate for the pasta, use a filled-in circle. Then add squiggles for the pasta.

Duplicate the first costume and add marinara sauce for the second costume. (Draw a closed-off shape and fill it in for the sauce.)

Duplicate the second costume and add cheese for the final cooked spaghetti costume. (Add dots for the cheese using the pencil tool.)

Name the costumes *plated pasta*, *pasta sauce*, and *finished*.

STEP 12: Place the clock and cooked spaghetti on the appropriate backdrops. (To do this, select the backdrop in the backdrop section, then drag the sprite to the correct spot on your creation screen. When you are finished, name the backdrops *clock* and *cooked spaghetti*.

Don't worry if there are other sprites on the screen when you do this. You'll code them to disappear on screens you don't want them on later.)

Steps:

3. wait 8-12 minutes for the spaghetti to cook in boiling water

4. Drain spaghetti from water.

Steps:

5. Place spaghetti on a plate with marinara sauce and cheese.

ENJOY!

STEP 13: Add this code to the *cooked spaghetti* sprite.

These blocks tell the sprite when to hide and show, depending on the step. The longer code with the repeat block animates the sprite by switching through its costumes.

If you'd like the pasta to switch through the costumes faster, change the wait time to a smaller number!

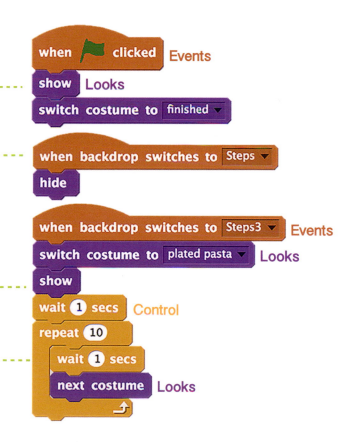

STEP 14: Add the below code to the *clock* sprite.

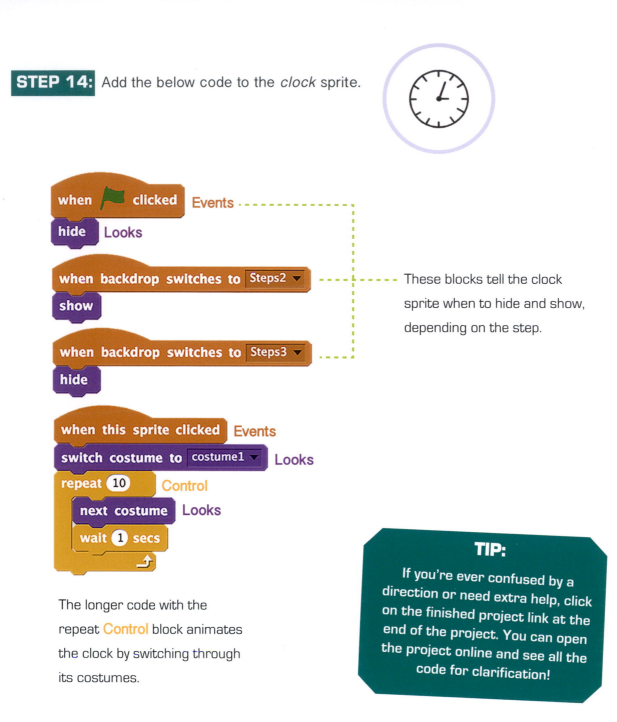

These blocks tell the clock sprite when to hide and show, depending on the step.

The longer code with the repeat Control block animates the clock by switching through its costumes.

TIP:

If you're ever confused by a direction or need extra help, click on the finished project link at the end of the project. You can open the project online and see all the code for clarification!

You're ready to teach people how to make spaghetti! View your finished project and use the space bar to move through the steps. See the finished project here: https://scratch.mit.edu/projects/174294795/

THE PROJECT:

Click the space bar to start the quiz. Click on the answer you think is correct—if you're wrong, an *X* will appear. If you get it right, a check mark will appear, and the test will move on to the next question. You have one minute to answer all the questions correctly. Think you have what it takes?

This quiz uses very simple questions. Before creating your own quiz, think about what you'd like the theme to be. Is it a quiz for something you're learning about in school? Or maybe it's about your favorite movie or TV show. The choice is up to you!

LET'S GET STARTED!

STEP 1: Start a new project and delete Scratch Cat. Then open the Background Library and select the stripes background. In vector mode, use the text icon to add your own quiz message to the background. (Make sure you mention pressing the space bar to begin.) Name this background *Start Page*.

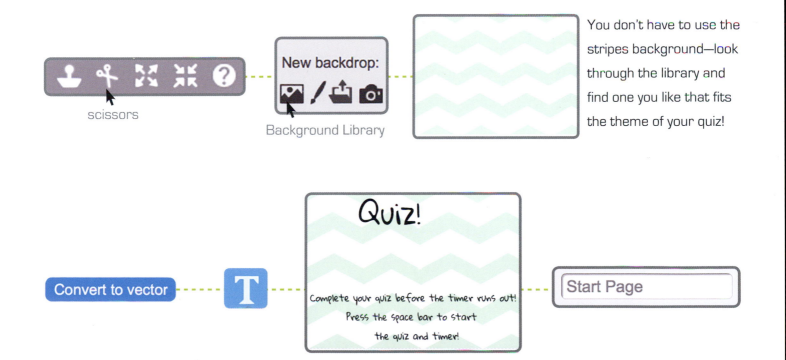

scissors

Background Library

You don't have to use the stripes background—look through the library and find one you like that fits the theme of your quiz!

Convert to vector

Quiz!

Complete your quiz before the timer runs out!
Press the space bar to start
the quiz and timer!

Start Page

STEP 2: After you've decided on your theme, think about the questions you'd like to ask. This example only has four questions, but you can use as many as you'd like!

 Use the stamp tool to duplicate your *start page* and use the text tool to add your question to the screen. (Make sure you are still in *vector mode* so you can easily change the question for the rest of your backgrounds.) Name this background *Q1*.

Once you have finished the *Q1* background, use the stamp tool to duplicate it and create the *Q2* backdrop. You can also right click on the *Q1* background in your backdrops toolbar on the left and select *Duplicate*.

Continue duplicating and changing questions until you have a total of four questions—or however many you need for your quiz.

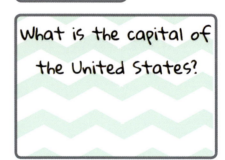

STEP 3: Create two final backgrounds—a *Time's Up* background and a *Win* background. You can make them look however you'd like, but be sure to name them!

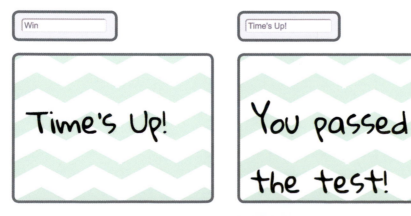

STEP 4: Go to the Scripts tab (for any sprite) and open the **Data** category. Click *Make a Variable* to create a new variable and name it *timer*. You will have access to the **Data** blocks.

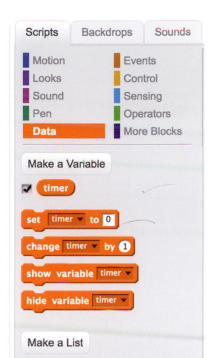

STEP 5: Add this code to the backdrop under the Scripts tab.

when [flag] clicked — Events
switch backdrop to Start Page — Looks
set timer to 60 — Data

when space key pressed — Events
switch backdrop to Q 1 — Looks
forever — Control
  wait 1 secs
  change timer by -1 — Data
  if ⟨ timer = 0 ⟩ then — Data/Operators
    switch backdrop to Time's Up! — Looks
    stop all — Control

This code starts the quiz when the green flag is clicked. The backdrop will change to the start screen, and the timer will be set to 60.

When the space bar is pressed, the backdrop switches to the *Q1* and then the quiz timer will forever wait one second and then count down by one. To end the game, the timer must equal zero. At that point, the backdrop switches to *Time's Up* and the timer stops counting down.

- - - - - - - Build this block using the *equals* block from **Operators** and the timer variable from **Data**. Then drag it into your larger **Control** block.

STEP 6: In the *New sprite* toolbar, click on the paintbrush to draw a new sprite. (Convert to vector mode before going further). Use the text tool to type in one answer option for your first question. In the sprite's info section, name it *Q1_A* (question one, option A).

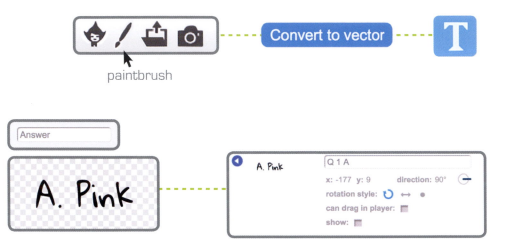

paintbrush

Name the first costume of this sprite answer. Then duplicate the costume and draw an *X* or check mark through it, depending on if it's the right or wrong answer. Name it *wrong* or *correct*, depending on which one it is. Then open the *Q1* background and drag the answer sprite to the location of your choice.

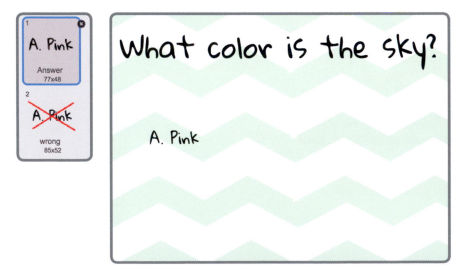

STEP 7: Add the code below to the *Q1_A* sprite. (This code is for an incorrect answer.)

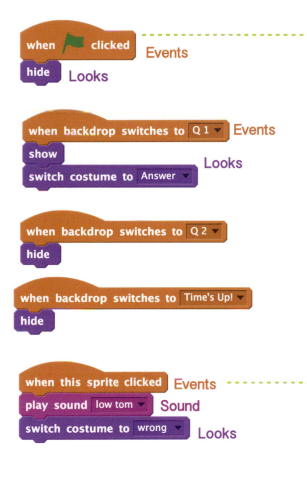

Since this is for *Q1*, the code tells the sprite that when the green flag is clicked, it should hide, the backdrop should switch to *Q2*, or the backdrop should switch to *Time's Up!* . Then it is directed to show when the backdrop switches to *Q1*.

When the sprite is clicked, a sound will play, and the costume will switch to *wrong*. Make sure you selected the sound you want from the Sound Library—otherwise you won't be able to select it here. (We used *low tom* and *cheer.*)

STEP 8: Use the stamp tool at the top to duplicate the *Q1_A* sprite three times. You should now have four possible answers. Open each sprite's information and rename them according to option: *Q1_B*, *Q1_C*, or *Q1_D*. In the Costumes section of each, change the letters and answers to match the sprite's new name.

A. Pink	B. Green	C. Blue	D. Yellow
Q 1 A	Q 1 B	Q 1 C	Q 1 D

Make sure all the sprites are named like this!

When you are changing the costumes for all the *Q1* sprites, make sure that one of the answer choices is correct. The second costume for the correct answer should be named *correct*, and it should have a green check mark over it. (For this question, sprite *Q1_C* has the correct answer costume.)

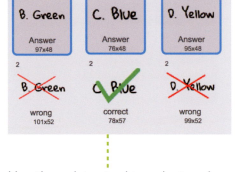

Duplicating the *Q1_A* sprite means all the code that you created on that sprite duplicated as well. Now the code is the same for all the wrong answer sprites and almost the same for the correct answer sprite.

Use the pointer tool to select and delete the red X before using the pencil tool to add the green check mark.

The sprite with the correct costume should have its code changed from what you see on the left to the code on the right. (The code block on the left will already be in the Scripts tab thanks to your earlier duplication.)

```
when this sprite clicked
play sound  low tom ▼
switch costume to  wrong ▼
```
→
```
when this sprite clicked
switch costume to  correct ▼
play sound  cheer ▼  until done
switch backdrop to  Q 2 ▼
```

These two pieces of code are very similar. But since the code on the right is going on the correct answer sprite, you want the correct answer to move the player to the next question. Instead of just showing the wrong costume, this sprite needs to show the correct costume, play the cheer sound, and switch to *Q2*.

The following steps will be very similar to steps 7 and 8. You will be creating answer sprites for the different question backgrounds. (Keep in mind that your questions may differ from what you see here, so your answers might be different too.) Keep naming your sprites using the question number and answer letter (Example: *Q1_A*) to avoid confusion since there will be a lot of sprites being used!

TIP:

To transfer code you've created from one sprite to another without duplication, use your mouse and click on the very first block (the start command). Then drag the whole code block onto the sprite in the Sprite section (so your mouse is in the middle of the sprite), and let go. The code you dragged will spring back to where you grabbed it from, and an exact copy will now be on the sprite you moved it to!

STEP 9: Use the stamp tool to duplicate one of the sprites from step 7 four times. (This way you don't have to recreate the entire set of code; you'll just change a few things.) In the information section, change the names of the new sprites to *Q2_A*, *Q2_B*, *Q2_C*, and *Q2_D*. Edit the costumes to reflect the answers that go with question 2. (Don't forget to change the wrong costume to correct on the correct answer!)

Go back to your backdrops and click on *Q2*. Drag the sprites to the correct spots on the question screen. (You might need to hide the other sprites temporarily to make it easier. To do this, open the information tab on the *Q1* sprites and uncheck the show box on each.) Make sure you do the same thing for your *Q1* backdrop and sprites.

What is the capital of the United States?

A. Washington, D.C.   C. New York

B. Las Vegas   D. Miami

STEP 10: Since the code from the *Q1* answer sprites was duplicated onto the *Q2* sprites, you will need to adjust the code slightly. Go into the Scripts tab of your *Q2* sprites to tweak the existing code blocks until it matches what you see here.

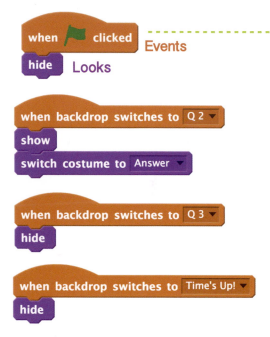

This code tells the *Q2* answer choices when to show and hide. The answer choice sprites will hide when the green flag is clicked and when the backdrop switches to *Q3*. The code will show and switch the sprite to the answer costume when the backdrop switches to *Q2*.

Pick which code is appropriate, depending on if this is a correct or incorrect answer choice. If you are adding code to the wrong answer sprite, add the wrong answer code, which will play the *low tom* sound and switch the costume to *wrong* when the sprite is clicked. If it is the correct answer choice, add the code that switches the costume to *correct*, plays the *cheer* sound, and switches the backdrop to *Q3* when the sprite is clicked.

WRONG ANSWER CODE: ## RIGHT ANSWER CODE:

Repeat steps 9 and 10 to create the answer sprites for *Q3* and *Q4*. The code for the *Q3* sprites will be the same as what you see above, except it will show when the backdrop switches to *Q3* and hide when backdrop switches to *Q4*.

The code for the final question (*Q4* in our quiz) will need to switch the backdrop to *winner* to end the quiz. The code will look like this for the *Q4* sprites:

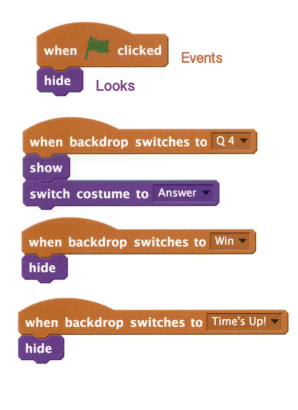

Choose between the last two codes, depending on if it's a correct or incorrect answer.

RIGHT ANSWER CODE:

WRONG ANSWER CODE:

You're ready to stump people with your quiz! View your completed project and click the space bar to start the quiz! Click on the answer you think is correct. If you're wrong, an *X* will appear. If you got the question right, a check mark will appear. You have one minute to answer all the questions correctly! See the finished project here:
https://scratch.mit.edu/projects/174307523/

Part 3

Musical Projects and Makey Makey

How to Use the Sound Tools

Adding sound to your projects is a great way to customize your creations. Scratch has tons of built-in options, but there are also fun ways to create and edit your own sounds. You can even upload them!

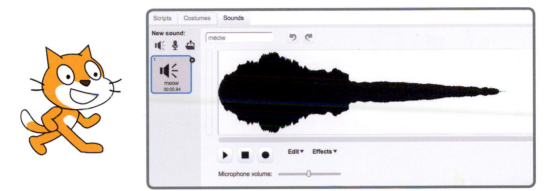

Above is the Sounds section for Scratch Cat. Each sprite comes with one sound preloaded. For Scratch Cat it's *meow*. (Makes sense, huh?) When you select a sound, you will see the length of the sound in the area to the right. You can use the edit tools to shorten the sounds and the effects option to customize the sound slightly. (We'll talk about how to do this later.)

The easiest way to add a sound to a project is to select it from the Sound Library. To access the Sound Library, click on the icon that looks like a speaker. When the library opens, you can sort the sounds by category and/or alphabetically.

New sound:

Sound Library

Category
All
Animal
Effects
Electronic
Human
Instruments
Music Loops
Musical Notes
Percussion
Vocals

To preview a sound, click on it, then click the play button. To select the sound for your project, click *OK* on the bottom right.

beat box2   bell cymbal   bell toll   bird   birthday bells

cave   chee chee   cheer   chomp   chord

cough-male   crash beatbox   crash cymbal   cricket   crickets

There are a few options for sound choices other than selecting one from the Sound Library. If you click the icon that looks like a microphone, you can record your own sound. A new sound (labeled: *recording 1*) will appear in your list of sounds.

To start recording your sound, click on the circle button.

The first time you do this, you'll see a message that looks like this:

Clicking *Allow* will cause a sound box to appear.

When you are recording, the circle will turn red and a message that says *Recording . . .* will appear. To stop recording, click the square button. When you click stop, the sound you just recorded will fill the sound space.

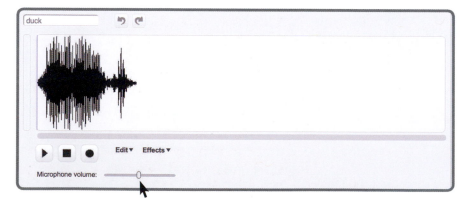

If the sound you were trying to record wasn't picked up, try adjusting the microphone volume on the slider bar.

You can also upload a sound from your computer. Make sure it's an mp3 or wav file. You can find a lot of sounds online, but not all are free or easy to download—www.soundbible.com is a good place to look. This website lets you search through thousands of sounds. Use the search bar to help you find the sound you're looking for.

Similar Sound Effects	Listen	License
Wetlands	▶	Attribution 3.0
Radar Detector Beeps	▶	Personal Use Only
Spear Throw	▶	Attribution 3.0
Vintage Phone Ringing	▶	Sampling Plus 1.0
Large Servo Motor	▶	Attribution 3.0
Sound Effect	Listen	License

Once you've started a search, a list of sounds will appear. You can preview the sounds using the play button.

When you find a sound you like, click on the name to download it. Then click the music note icon labeled *MP3*.

Now that you've downloaded the sound to your computer, click on the upload icon—the one that looks like a folder with an arrow—within the new sound panel. A window will open giving you access to the files on your computer. Open the downloads section and find your MP3 file. Select the file, then click *open* at the bottom of the screen.

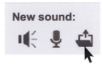

Here you can see the sound properly uploaded into Scratch. The download name will automatically appear in the sound name box. To change it, just click inside and rename it. Since you downloaded the sound, be sure to give credit to its creator in your project description.

The file should upload straight into the Sounds tab on Scratch.

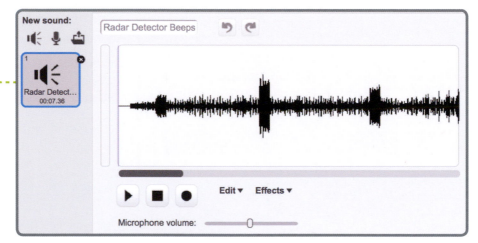

TIP:

If you get an error message, try uploading one more time, or changing the download type. (Example: If you tried downloading and uploading a WAV file, try downloading and uploading the MP3 file instead.)

EDIT AND EFFECTS

Any sound in Scratch can be changed using the Edit and/or Effects tools. (For this example, we've selected the birthday sound from the Sound Library.) To start, select the portion of the sound you want to edit by highlighting it with your mouse.

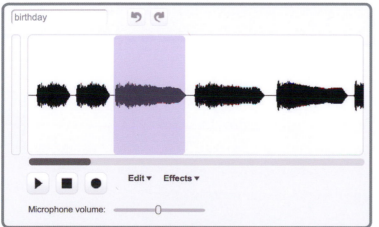

We've chosen the beginning of the birthday sound. Click on the arrows next to *Edit* and *Effects* to see your options. You can make that portion louder, softer, or silent. If you want to shorten a sound, select *everything except* the part you want to keep. Then use the *cut* option in the *Edit* menu so only the section you want is remaining.

TIP:

If you make a mistake, use *undo* or *redo* in the Edit menu, or use the undo or redo arrows next to the sound name.

Rainbow Piano

THE PROJECT:

Create a piano that changes colors when each key plays a note. Whether you are a pianist or just like pressing random keys, this project is a rainbow of sound!

LET'S GET STARTED!

STEP 1: Start a new project and delete Scratch Cat. (Don't forget to name your project!) Use the paintbrush in the new backdrop toolbar to create a new backdrop. It should look something like this:

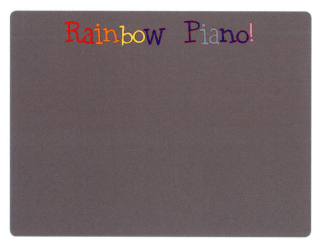

 Use the paint bucket to fill in the background with a solid color of your choice. (A dark color is good so that the rainbow piano keys don't blend in when they are played.)

 Use the text tool to type in *Rainbow Piano!* (You can choose whatever font you'd like at the bottom of the screen.) Make the font larger by stretching the text box with the sizing dots.

 Use the paint bucket to change the color of your rainbow letters.

STEP 2: Click on the paintbrush icon in the sprite toolbar to draw a new sprite. (Make sure you convert to vector mode before you start drawing!)

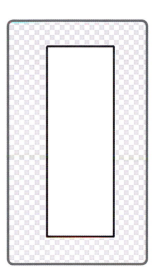

Look at the bottom right of the page for this. **Convert to vector**

Once you click *Convert to vector*, your drawing tools will be on the right side of the screen and will look like this: ⟶

Use the square tool to draw a rectangle outlined in black.

Use the paint bucket to fill in the rectangle with white.

`key`

In the top left corner, name this first costume *key*.

STEP 3: Duplicate the *key* costume using the stamp tool at the top of the screen. You should now have two costumes on the same sprite.

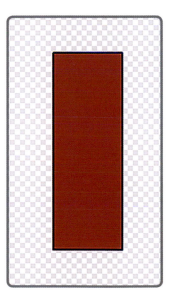

Use the paint bucket to fill in the second key with a color of your choice.

`colored key`

In the top left corner, change the name of the new costume to *colored key*. (It's important to always name your costumes. This will make it easier to code changes between them.)

STEP 4: Add this code to the Scripts tab of your sprite:

Use the arrow to select the costume name from the dropdown menu. (If you didn't name your costumes in the earlier steps, the names won't match. Double check those!)

```
when this sprite clicked         Events
switch costume to  colored key ▼    Looks
play note 60▼ for 0.5 beats       Sound
wait 0.2 secs    Control
switch costume to  key ▼
                  Looks
```

This section of code is activated when the sprite is clicked.

Then the costume switches to the colored key, a note plays, there's a 0.2 second wait, and the costume switches back to the first *key* costume.

If you want the colored key to stay on the screen longer, increase the wait time. Click on the arrow to open the dropdown menu and select the note for your *key* sprite. Start with *Middle C (60)* for this sprite.

STEP 5: Duplicate your sprite (not the costume!) 12 times. (Use the stamp tool at the top of the screen.) You should have 13 sprites at the end of this step.

stamp

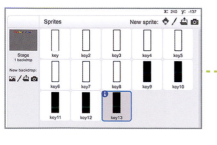

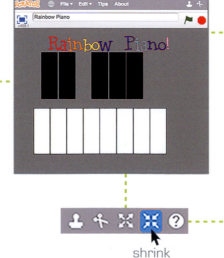

shrink

Arrange eight keys together in a line and place five keys on top.

Go into the Costumes tabs for the five sprites on top and use the paint bucket to make them all black.

Shrink and move the five black keys to finish your piano arrangement! Using the *shrink* tool, click the sprites until they are the right size.

STEP 6: In the Costumes tabs of all the white key sprites, use the paint bucket to change the color of the *colored key* costume. Here are the Costume sections for our white keys:

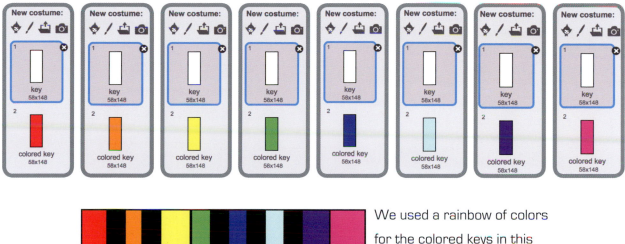

We used a rainbow of colors for the colored keys in this project, but you can pick whatever colors you'd like!

STEP 7: To change the color of the black keys, open the Costumes section of each sprite. Select the *colored key* costume and use the paint bucket and a mixture of two colors to create a cool effect.

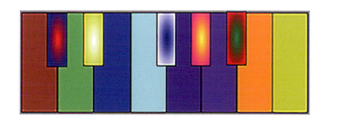

Click the paint bucket. Select the two colors you want to mix together.

Select how you'd like to mix them. Use the paint bucket to fill in the key.

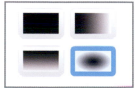

STEP 8: Because you duplicated your original sprite, each of the key sprites already has this duplicated code. Now you need to change the note each sprite plays.

Double click on the key you need to change. Then open the Scripts tab and find the *play note* block. Open the dropdown menu in the **Sound** block and choose the note that matches the key on your piano. (For this sprite, it would be D.) Change this code block for all your piano keys so they play the correct note.

Note: You'll only use the last 13 keys on the keyboard in the *play note* code block.

STEP 9: Tweak the code on the black keys so they stay on top of the white keys. The only block you're adding is the *go to front* block from **Looks**. You also need to change the note for each black key in the *play note* block. Do that the same way you did for the white keys in step 8.

This code places the black keys in front of the white keys. When a black key is pressed, it changes its costume to *colored key*, plays the correct note, waits a moment, and then changes back to the regular key costume.

Go to your finished project screen to play your piano and watch the keys change color! See the finished project here:

https://scratch.mit.edu/projects/173770364/

TIP:

If the piano keys aren't changing color properly, go into Scripts and re-select the costume they need to switch to.

THE PROJECT:

Click on the different instruments to hear the beach band play! To hear all the instruments at once, click the *play all* button.

LET'S GET STARTED!

STEP 1: Start and name your new project. Delete Scratch Cat, then click on the mountain landscape icon in the *New backdrop* toolbar to open the Backdrop Library. Select a beach background for your band to play on.

scissors

Backdrop Library

STEP 2: Open the Sprite Library and choose the instrument sprites you'd like for your band. (Repeat until you have as many as you want.) Then select a person sprite so you have someone to dance to the music!

Theme
Castle
City
Dance
Dress-Up
Flying
Holiday
Music
Space
Sports
Underwater
Walking

- - - - - Narrow down your options to sprites in the music category (on the left side of the library) to make it easier to find what you need.

Sprite Library

Catherine...   Cymbal   Drum1   Piano   Saxophone

STEP 3: Arrange all the sprites on the backdrop as shown. Click and drag the sprites to move them around your screen. (You might need to use the shrink button to make all your instruments fit.)

STEP 4: Add the below code to the Scripts section of your person sprite to make him/her move. Then open the sprite's information box (by clicking on the small ⓘ) and change the rotation style to right-to-left so the sprite doesn't flip upside down when moving.

This sprite comes with dancing costumes, which makes coding the animation easy. All your sprite needs to do is wait a small amount of time—so it doesn't move too quickly—move a bit, and change costumes!

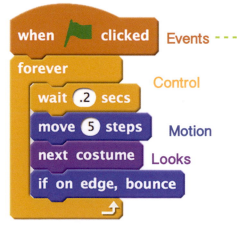

This code starts when the green flag is clicked. The sprite will forever move, switch costumes (making it look like it's dancing), and wait a moment before repeating again. The *if on edge bounce* block prevents the sprite from moving off the screen when it gets to the edge.

STEP 5: Select a button sprite from the Sprite Library. In the Costumes tab, use the text tool to add the words *play all* to the button.

```
when this sprite clicked
broadcast  Play ▼
```
Events - - - - - - - - Then add this code to the Scripts section of the button sprite. You will need to create a new message for the play broadcast.

STEP 6: Add the below code to the piano sprite. If you play piano, are musical, or just want to get creative, feel free to change the notes to a combination that you like. Otherwise just copy the notes you see here!

```
when this sprite clicked     Events
set tempo to (60) bpm        Sound
repeat (10)                  Control
    play note (60▼) for (0.5) beats
    play note (64▼) for (0.5) beats
    play note (67▼) for (0.5) beats
play note (67▼) for (0.5) beats
play note (64▼) for (0.5) beats
play note (60▼) for (0.5) beats
```

This code is activated when the piano sprite is clicked. But you also want the piano to play when the *play all* button is pressed and the *play* broadcast is received.

Use the stamp tool to duplicate the entire code block. Then (on the duplicate) pull off everything below the start command. Discard the original start command and add a *when I receive play* block to the top. The code under both start commands will be identical.

```
when I receive  Play ▼     Events
set tempo to (60) bpm       Sound
repeat (10)                 Control
    play note (60▼) for (0.5) beats
    play note (64▼) for (0.5) beats
    play note (67▼) for (0.5) beats
play note (67▼) for (0.5) beats
play note (64▼) for (0.5) beats
play note (60▼) for (0.5) beats
```

The numbers in the *play note* block represent the note's pitch. Pitch is how high or low a note is. The higher the number, the higher the pitch!

To select the proper note, click on the arrow to open the keyboard.

```
play note (60▼) for (0.5) beats
```

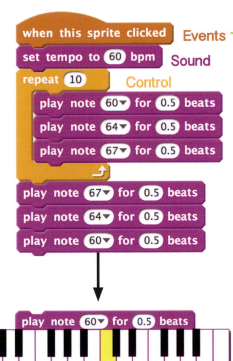

Middle C (60)

STEP 7: Add both code blocks from step 6 to the saxophone sprite. (The first one will be identical to the code on the piano except for the first **Sound** block.) Don't forget to change instrument to *saxophone* in that block.

Click the arrow to open the drop-down menu and select the instrument.

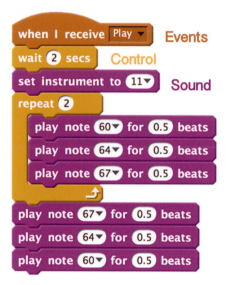

The second set of code will also need a *wait* command before the sounds play. (This will tell the instruments to start in rounds when they play together.) Add a wait command (2 seconds) below the *when I receive play* start command. Then change the *set tempo to* block to *set instrument to*. Don't forget to change the instrument to saxophone!

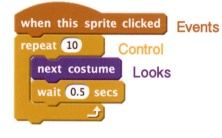

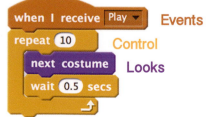

Add these two new blocks to the saxophone's Scripts tab. (The blocks are identical, except for their start commands, so it's easy to create one, duplicate it with the stamp tool, and swap out the first block.) These tell the sprite to switch costumes when clicked or when the *play* broadcast is received.

TIP:
You can copy the code blocks from the piano sprite to your saxophone sprite to save time. Just use your mouse pointer to select the entire code block you want to copy and drag it to hover over your saxophone sprite. When you let go, the code will bounce back to the Scripts section and be loaded to the saxophone.

There will be a total of four code blocks on the saxophone when you are finished with step 7—two with the *play* broadcast start command and two with the *sprite clicked* start command. Running two sets of code under the same start command is called **parallel processing**. This is used when you need two things to start and run at the same time.

STEP 8: Add this code to the cymbal sprite. Since the cymbal automatically comes with another costume, you will use parallel processing again to make the sprite play sounds and switch costumes when it's clicked.

Use the stamp tool to duplicate the top two code blocks. Then swap out the *when this sprite clicked* start commands for the *when I receive* start commands from **Events**. You should have four code blocks on the cymbal at the end of step 8.

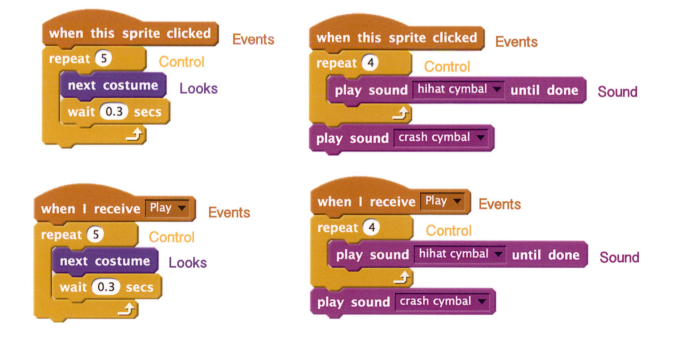

The cymbal sounds are already in the Sounds tab for this sprite, so you don't need to add them.

STEP 9: Add this code to one of the *drum* sprites. Then use the stamp tool to duplicate the code. On the duplicate, swap out the start command for the *when I receive play* start command and add a one-second wait block from **Control**.

These blocks tell the drum sprite to play the selected notes—choose what you'd like or use what's shown here. Some notes will repeat if you add a loop. Get creative and make a beat all your own using the *play note* blocks from **Sound**.

when this sprite clicked **Events**
repeat 5 **Control**
play drum 1▾ for 1 beats

when I receive Play▾ **Events**
repeat 5 **Control**
play drum 1▾ for 1 beats **Sound**

STEP 10: Add this code to the second drum sprite.

when this sprite clicked **Events**
set tempo to 60 bpm
set instrument to 18▾ **Sound**
repeat 2 **Control**
  play note 60▾ for 0.5 beats
  play note 64▾ for 0.5 beats
  play note 67▾ for 0.5 beats
play note 67▾ for 0.5 beats
play note 64▾ for 0.5 beats
play note 60▾ for 0.5 beats

when I receive Play▾ **Events**
wait 1 secs **Control**
set tempo to 60 bpm
set instrument to 18▾ **Sound**
repeat 2
  play note 60▾ for 0.5 beats
  play note 64▾ for 0.5 beats
  play note 67▾ for 0.5 beats
play note 67▾ for 0.5 beats
play note 64▾ for 0.5 beats
play note 60▾ for 0.5 beats

Go to your finished project screen to see your band in action! Click the green flag, then press on the individual instruments to hear them play, or press the *play all* button to hear them all play together and watch your person dance! See the finished project here:

https://scratch.mit.edu/projects/174112647/

THE PROJECT:

Watch as the ghost flies through a starry sky. See what happens when you make a loud sound and scare the ghost!

LET'S GET STARTED!

STEP 1: Start a new project and delete Scratch Cat. (Make sure to name and save your project!) In your backdrop screen, create a dark night sky and a small amount of grass/ground at the bottom.

scissors

New backdrop:

paintbrush

Use the paint bucket tool to fill in the sky black.

Use the filled-in green rectangle to make a small patch of ground on the bottom of the backdrop. Don't worry about drawing the stars—those will be added later as sprites.

STEP 2: Open the Sprite Library and select *Ghost1*.

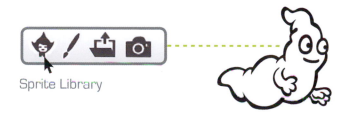

Sprite Library

STEP 3: Use the paintbrush icon in the new sprite toolbar to create a new sprite. Before you go any further, click *Convert to vector* at the bottom of the screen. Then follow these steps to draw a pumpkin sprite:

paintbrush

Use the circle tool to draw a filled-in orange circle.

 Click the reshape icon, then click on the orange circle to make the reshape dots appear. Move the sizing dots around to create a pumpkin-like shape. Pull the top dot down a bit. Then pull the bottom dots out to create a flatter bottom.

 Use the pencil tool and the color brown to draw lines on the pumpkin. Then use the square tool to draw a little stem on the top of the pumpkin.

When you're finished, open the sprite's information and name it *pumpkin*. Then change the rotation style to the right-to-left rotation.

STEP 4: Use the paintbrush icon to create a new sprite. Then use the paintbrush tool to draw a cluster of five to eight stars. (You might need to change the thickness of the paintbrush at the bottom of the screen.) Make sure you draw the stars close to the little cross in the drawing section; don't spread them out too much!

Name this sprite *stars*. Select the right-to-left rotation style in its information section.

STEP 5: Add the below code to the Scripts sections of both the *pumpkin* and *stars* sprites. This will make it look like the stars and the pumpkin are scrolling across the screen.

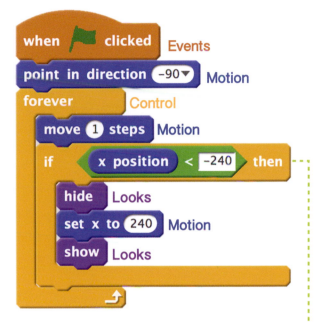

Use a *less than* block from **Operators** and a **Motion** block to build this piece of code. Then drop it inside your larger **Control** block.

When the green flag is clicked, the sprites face the left of the screen. Then they will forever move one step, and if their X positions become less than -240 (the farthest spot on the left of the screen), the sprites will hide, set X to 240 (the farthest spot on the right of the screen), and show back up. They will continue moving, getting to the end of the screen, hiding, repositioning, and showing as long as the project is playing!

TIP:
You can build this code block on one sprite and copy it to the other sprite to save time. (See page 136 if you need a reminder on how to do this.)

STEP 6: Use the stamp tool at the top of the screen to duplicate the *stars* and *pumpkin* sprites until you have three stars sprites and four pumpkin sprites. (These duplicates will already have all the code you added in step 5.) When you're finished, arrange the sprites on the screen as shown. (Use the shrink or grow tools at the top to adjust the size of the pumpkins so they're not all identical.)

STEP 7: Add the below code to the Scripts section of your ghost sprite. Since the sprites around the ghost will be moving, this will create the illusion that the ghost is flying through the air. In reality, the ghost will just bounce up and down in place!

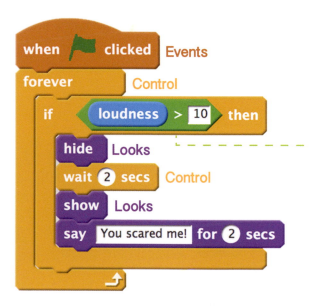

When the green flag is clicked, the ghost sprite will forever glide from the center of the screen (x:0 y:0) to a spot slightly above it (x:0 y:10). This makes the ghost look like it's flying!

When the green flag is clicked, if the loudness is greater than 10, then the ghost will forever hide for two seconds, then show and say, *You scared me!* (You can adjust the loudness number to be more or less sensitive if needed.)

Use a *greater than* block from **Operators** and the *loudness* block from **Sensing** to build this piece of code. Then drop it inside your larger **Control** block. When you pull the *loudness* block out of **Sensing**, you will be asked to allow access to the microphone. Make sure you press *Allow*. This will let you interact with the ghost using sounds you make!

Extras: To make the stars change color as they scroll across the screen, add the *change color effect by __* block to your stars sprite(s). To make the colors change faster, increase the number.

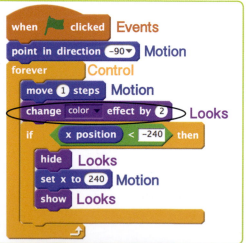

Go to your finished project screen and click the green flag to start. Watch as the ghost flies through the sky—see what happens if you make a loud noise. See the finished project here: https://scratch.mit.edu/projects/174317731/

THE PROJECT:

Set the tempo of the ball to see how quickly it moves. What happens to the ball if you increase the tempo?

LET'S GET STARTED!

STEP 1: Start a new project, and delete Scratch Cat. Create a new backdrop, and use the paint bucket tool to fill in the background with a solid color. Use the square tool (not filled in) to create an outline around the edges of your backdrop in a different solid color.

scissors   New backdrop: paintbrush

STEP 2: Open the Sprite Library and select the ball sprite. Then go to the sprite's Costumes tab and use the paint bucket to change the color of the ball. (Or select a ball from the different costumes already attached to the sprite.)

Sprite Library

STEP 3: Open the Sprite Library again and select the button sprite. In the Costumes tab, use the paint bucket to change the button's color and use the text tool to add the words *Change Tempo*.

CHANGE TEMPO

STEP 4: Go to the button sprite's Scripts tab and navigate to the **Data** category. Click *make a variable* and name it *tempo*. (We'll need this variable later in the project.)

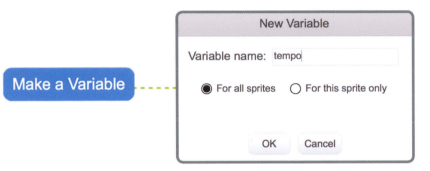

STEP 5: Add the below code to the button sprite. Then open the sprite's information section and name it *tempo*.

```
when this sprite clicked    Events
ask  What would you like the tempo to be?  and wait   Sensing
set  Tempo ▾  to  answer    Data / Sensing
```

The *ask and wait* code block lets you incorporate user input into your project. When this button is pressed, a bar will pop up that lets the user type in what they want the tempo to be. The *tempo* variable will then be set to that answer.

WHAT IS TEMPO?

Tempo refers to the speed of music being played. It is sometimes referred to as the beat! Listen to the beat the ball makes as it touches the edges and plays the pop sound. That's the ball's tempo.

Add the below code blocks to the ball sprite.

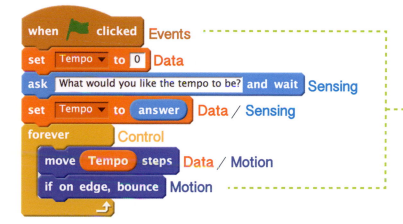

This code tells the ball sprite to move from side to side on the screen at a certain speed. When the green flag is clicked, the tempo is set to zero, and the user is asked to set the tempo. Once the tempo is set, the ball will forever move that number of steps and bounce off the edges.

The code tells the ball sprite to play the *pop* sound when it touches the outline on the screen. The code is activated when the green flag is clicked. Forever, if the ball touches the color blue and the tempo is less than 10, the *pop* sound will play and there will be a one-second wait. (This is so the sound doesn't play twice when the ball is going over the color blue.)

There is no wait block on the bottom section of code because when the tempo is higher, the ball will move faster. You don't have to worry about the *pop* sound playing twice.

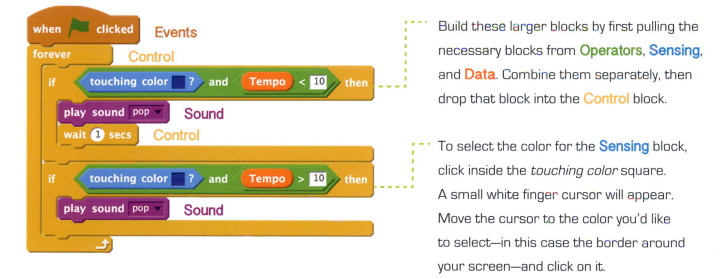

Build these larger blocks by first pulling the necessary blocks from **Operators**, **Sensing**, and **Data**. Combine them separately, then drop that block into the **Control** block.

To select the color for the **Sensing** block, click inside the *touching color* square. A small white finger cursor will appear. Move the cursor to the color you'd like to select—in this case the border around your screen—and click on it.

Go to your finished project screen to see your game in action. Click the flag to start, then set and change the tempo of the ball to see how quickly it moves. See the finished project here:
https://scratch.mit.edu/projects/174318688/

Soundboard

THE PROJECT:

Click the different buttons to hear the sounds or pictures they represent! Record your own sounds, use sounds from Scratch, or upload new sounds to create the best soundboard ever!

LET'S GET STARTED!

STEP 1: Create and name a new project. Delete Scratch Cat, then use the paintbrush icon in your backdrop toolbar to create a new backdrop.

scissors

paintbrush

 Use the paint bucket to fill in the background with a solid color.

STEP 2: Use the paintbrush icon in your sprite toolbar to create a sprite that will describe how to use the soundboard. Use the text tool to add the words for the sprite. (Make sure your text is a different color from your background so it's visible!)

Click the buttons to hear the sounds and see the characters that go with them!

Sprite Library

TIP:
Sprites don't always have to be characters—sometimes they can be words, like what you see here!

STEP 3: Select eight button sprites from the Sprite Library. (You can also select one and use the stamp tool to duplicate it until you have the correct amount.) Name each sprite (in its Costume tab) using a sound you want in your soundboard. Then use the text tool to add the same word onto the sprite.

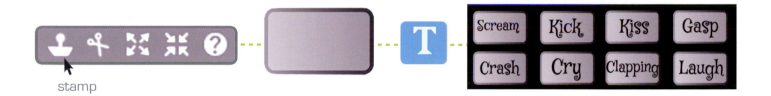

stamp

STEP 4: Select a sprite to go with each button. You can select the sprite from the Sprite Library, edit a sprite in the library, or create your own! You should have a total of 17 sprites at the end of this step: eight button sprites, eight characters to go with the buttons, and one text sprite. We chose to:

 Select *ghost2* from the Sprite Library.

Use the paintbrush icon (in bitmap mode) to create this sprite. Name it *crash*.

Select *heart face* from the Sprite Library.

Select *Pico walking* from the Sprite Library.

 Select *ballerina* from the Sprite Library. (This sprite comes with multiple costumes, so you can easily animate her to dance!)

 Use the paintbrush icon (in vector mode) to create this sprite. Name it *gasp*.

 Select *Hannah* from the Sprite Library.

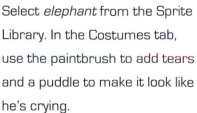 Select *elephant* from the Sprite Library. In the Costumes tab, use the paintbrush to add tears and a puddle to make it look like he's crying.

STEP 5: Arrange the button sprites to the backdrop as shown. Place the text sprite from step 2 next to the buttons. Then stack all the character sprites, one on top of the other, in the open space next to the buttons.

You will code the sprites to disappear and reappear at the correct time so they won't look cluttered when you are finished.

Use the grow/shrink tools to adjust the sizes of the sprites to your liking.

STEP 6: Open the Sound Library for each button sprite (except for *kiss* and *gasp*) and choose sounds to go with the buttons.

Sound Library

Sound Library

Category
All
Animal
Effects
Electronic
Human
Instruments
Music Loops
Musical Notes
Percussion
Vocals

Select the *Human* category to help find the sounds in the Sound Library. All the sounds needed for this step—except for kick drum, which is in the percussion category—can be found there.

Add the below code blocks to the *scream*, *crash*, *clapping*, *kick*, and *laugh* buttons. These codes will broadcast a message and make a sound when the sprite is pressed.

Be sure to create a new message for each broadcast using the drop-down menu. Name them to match the button.

STEP 7: There are no sounds in the Sound Library for *kiss* and *gasp* so you'll need to record those before adding the below code.

microphone

Click on the microphone in the Sounds tab of either sprite and record the correct sound. (Refer to *How to Use the Sound Tools* on page 123 if you need a refresher.)

After you've finished recording, you might need to use the edit tools. You can shorten your sound if it's too long, or make it louder if it's too quiet. When you're happy with your sound, change the name from *recording1* to either *kiss* or *gasp*. Repeat for other sounds.

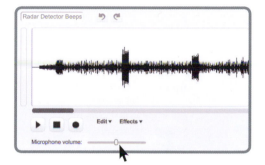

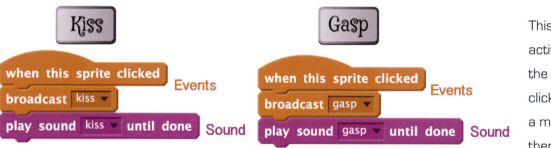

This code will activate when the buttons are clicked, broadcast a message, and then play a sound!

STEP 8: Next add the sound to the crying button sprite. You'll be uploading a sound* from your computer.

The crying sound for this project should only be a few seconds long. If the sound is too long, highlight the section of the sound that you need to remove and trim it. (For a refresher on how to use the edit tools, go page 127.) When you are done editing the sound, rename it *crying*.

> crying

*Don't forget to credit the sound's creator in your project. Below the download buttons is a list of information, including who recorded each sound. That's where you'll find who to credit.

STEP 9: Add this code to the crying button sprite:

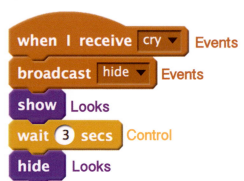

when this sprite clicked **Events**
broadcast cry ▼ **Events**
play sound crying ▼ until done **Sound**

Click the buttons to hear the sounds and see the characters that go with them!

STEP 10: Add this code to the text sprite:

when 🚩 clicked **Events**
show **Looks**

when I receive hide ▼ **Events** - - - - Create the new broadcast
hide **Looks**   using the dropdown menu.
wait 4 secs **Control**   The *hide* broadcast will
show **Looks**   be sent from the sound
                                                         character sprites.

STEP 11: Code each of the character sprites you see here with the below code blocks:

when 🚩 clicked **Events**
hide **Looks**

when I receive cry ▼ **Events**
broadcast hide ▼ **Events**
show **Looks**
wait 3 secs **Control**
hide **Looks**

This code will be the same on all the character sprites (except for *Pico* and *ballerina*). The only change in the code from sprite to sprite will be the start command. Make sure the start command matches with the character you're coding. (**Example:** The elephant sprite will start when it receives *cry*.)

Since *Pico* and *ballerina* have different costumes, which make them easy to animate, their code blocks will be slightly different. When they receive the appropriate broadcast, they will show, change costumes, and then hide. The repeat block tells the costumes to change a certain number of times (however many you put inside the repeat loop), and the wait block makes sure the costumes don't change too quickly.

Make sure the start command for Pico is changed to *when I receive laugh*, and the switch costume says *Pico walk1*!

Go to your finished project page and click the green flag to start. Click on the different buttons to hear the matching sounds and see the matching characters! See the finished project here: https://scratch.mit.edu/projects/174315736/

What Is Makey Makey?

Makey Makey is an awesome method for interacting with your computer in an original way. But what is it? Makey Makey is a type of user interface. A user interface is a way a person—a user—interacts with a computer. You're probably used to using basic user interfaces, like your computer's keyboard or mouse. But with Makey Makey, you can use objects like bananas, gummies, water, pencil lead, aluminum foil, flowers, or anything else that can conduct the smallest amount of electricity to control the arrow keys, space bar, and mouse click on your computer.

HERE'S WHAT COMES IN A MAKEY MAKEY KIT:

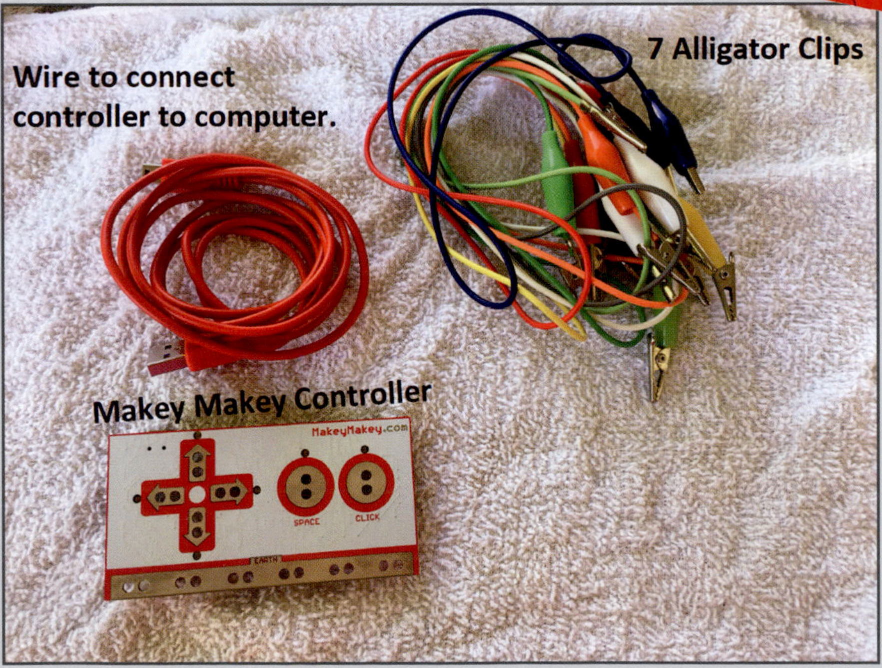

Wire to connect controller to computer.

7 Alligator Clips

Makey Makey Controller

Purchase a Makey Makey kit and check out some cool ways to use the Makey Makey here: https://www.makeymakey.com/

1. Connect the smaller end of the red wire to the matching opening on the back of the controller.

1. Connect the opposite end of the red wire to the USB port in your computer. Once it's successfully connected, the green lights on the controller will flash. A message may pop up on your computer asking you to verify the keyboard that was plugged in. (You don't need to install any software to use Makey Makey, so hit cancel on any pop-ups that appear.)

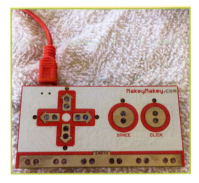

1. Makey Makey works by creating a **circuit** between your body and another conductive material—whatever you connect to using the alligator clips. Remember to connect an alligator clip to the earth section on the controller, and hold the other end of the clip with your fingers. This creates a complete circuit through your body when you touch something else. Keep reading to see what cool things you can attach and form a circuit with!

Earth Section

Hold it!

1. After you've connected to the earth section, start connecting the alligator clips to the other spots on the controller. (The controller corresponds to the arrow keys and space bar on your computer, as well as the mouse click/keypad.)

* **Circuit**—an electrical flow that starts and stops in the same place. (That same place will be the earth alligator clip for you!)

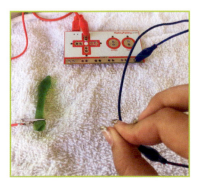

Here the blue alligator clip is connected to the earth section and someone's hand. The red clip is connected to a gummy worm and the up arrow. As long as the person stays connected to the earth section, the circuit will complete when the gummy worm is touched. Since the alligator clip is connected to the up arrow, whatever that arrow controls will now be controlled by the green gummy worm.

Think of all the projects you've created so far. Keep reading to see how you can control them using gummy worms and Play-Doh!

Gummy Worm Piano

THE PROJECT:

Use gummy worms to play the Rainbow Piano you created on page 128!

WHAT YOU'LL NEED:

- 4 gummy worms
- Makey Makey kit
- computer with Rainbow Piano Scratch project

TIP:

You can save a copy of your Rainbow Piano project so you can change the code without changing your original project. Just click on File and then save as a copy. (Change the name to something easy to remember, like Gummy Worm Piano.)

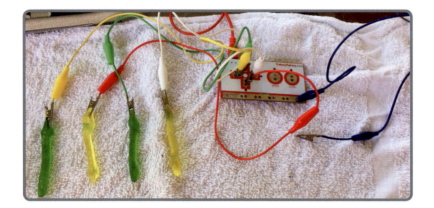

Arrange the gummy worms as shown in the photo, connecting one end of each alligator clip to a gummy and the other end to an arrow on the Makey Makey controller. This will let you control the up, down, left, and right arrows on your computer using the gummies. (Keep the alligator clips untangled so they don't get in your way when you start playing!) Make sure one alligator clip is always attached to earth and that you are holding the other end.

TIP:

If you'd like add a fifth gummy worm, attach it to the space bar position on the controller—the circle next to the arrow keys that says space.

Open the Rainbow Piano project you created earlier in this book. (That's why it's important to name and save all your work!) In that project, you played the piano by clicking on the keys using your mouse. To play your piano using Makey Makey and gummy worms, you'll need to change the start commands on the sprites to start commands that can be used through Makey Makey. (Remember, Makey Makey can be used with the arrow keys and space bar.) Change the code for all the piano key sprites so it matches what you see here:

Now when an arrow key is pressed, the sprite will switch its costume to the colored key, play a note for 0.5 beats, wait 0.2 seconds, and change its costume again.

Once you've edited your code blocks to work for Makey Makey, hold on to the earth alligator clip and tap the gummy worms to play the piano. When you tap the gummies (while holding earth) you are completing a circuit. The computer thinks you are touching the different arrow keys the gummies are connected to. Have fun!

Play-Doh Band

THE PROJECT:

Use Play-Doh balls to play instruments in the Beach Band project you created on page 133!

WHAT YOU'LL NEED:

- Play-Doh
- Makey Makey kit
- computer with Beach Band Scratch project

TIP:

Don't forget to save a copy of your project so you can make changes to the code without altering your original Beach Band.

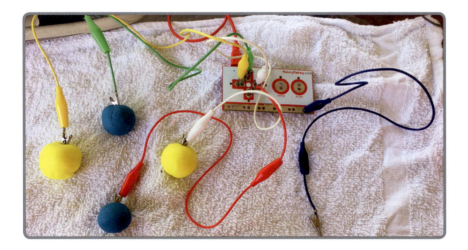

Create four small balls with your Play-Doh. Arrange them as shown, pushing one alligator clip firmly into each ball and connecting the other end of the clip to an arrow key on the Makey Makey controller. Make sure one alligator clip is always attached to earth and that you are holding the other end. Our example shows:

- white alligator clip/yellow Play-doh ball = right arrow
- green alligator clip/blue Play-Doh ball = up arrow
- red alligator clip/blue Play-Doh ball = down arrow
- yellow alligator clip/yellow Play-Doh ball = left arrow

TIP:

If you'd like add a fifth Play-Doh ball, attach it to the space bar position on the controller—the middle circle labeled space.

Open the Beach Band project you created earlier. In that project, you controlled the instruments using your mouse or by pressing the *play all* button. Now you'll need to change the start commands on the instrument and *play all* button sprites to commands that can be used through Makey Makey: the arrow keys and space bar. Change the code to match what you see here:

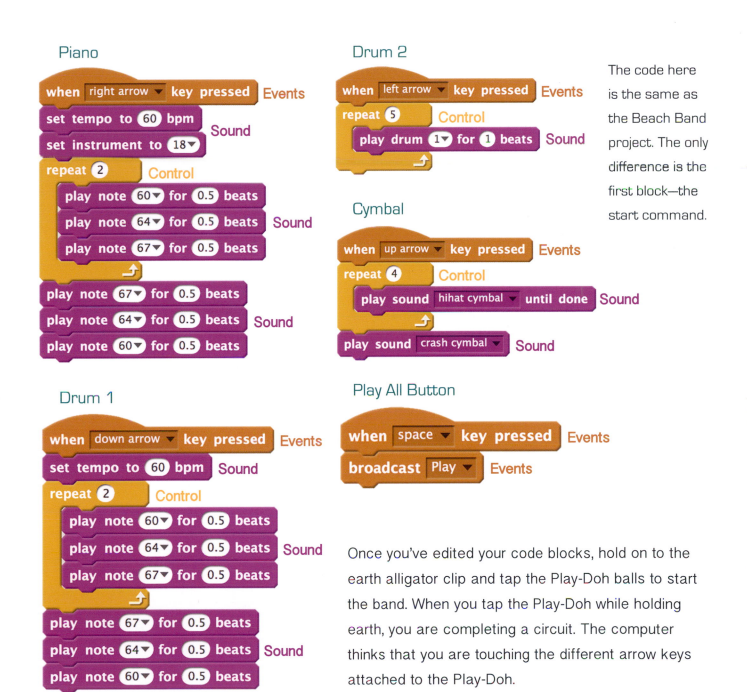

Piano

when [right arrow ▼] key pressed — Events
set tempo to (60) bpm — Sound
set instrument to (18▼)
repeat (2) — Control
    play note (60▼) for (0.5) beats
    play note (64▼) for (0.5) beats — Sound
    play note (67▼) for (0.5) beats
play note (67▼) for (0.5) beats
play note (64▼) for (0.5) beats — Sound
play note (60▼) for (0.5) beats

Drum 2

when [left arrow ▼] key pressed — Events
repeat (5) — Control
    play drum (1▼) for (1) beats — Sound

Cymbal

when [up arrow ▼] key pressed — Events
repeat (4) — Control
    play sound [hihat cymbal ▼] until done — Sound
play sound [crash cymbal ▼] — Sound

The code here is the same as the Beach Band project. The only difference is the first block—the start command.

Drum 1

when [down arrow ▼] key pressed — Events
set tempo to (60) bpm — Sound
repeat (2) — Control
    play note (60▼) for (0.5) beats
    play note (64▼) for (0.5) beats — Sound
    play note (67▼) for (0.5) beats
play note (67▼) for (0.5) beats
play note (64▼) for (0.5) beats — Sound
play note (60▼) for (0.5) beats

Play All Button

when [space ▼] key pressed — Events
broadcast [Play ▼] — Events

Once you've edited your code blocks, hold on to the earth alligator clip and tap the Play-Doh balls to start the band. When you tap the Play-Doh while holding earth, you are completing a circuit. The computer thinks that you are touching the different arrow keys attached to the Play-Doh.

Coding Glossary

bitmap mode: The design tools in this mode make it easy to fill in backgrounds and shapes. If you're making a quick shape or basic background, bitmap is a good choice. (Keep in mind that if you need to go back and resize a shape later, bitmap mode won't allow it.) To change between bitmap and vector mode, use the buttons on the bottom right of the design screen.

broadcast: A broadcast is like sending a message. For example, if you need one sprite to do something when another sprite is touched, you can send a message to it. Then set the start command on the second sprite to *when I receive* _____. (These code blocks can be found in the **Events** category.)

coding: The language used to communicate with a computer. By creating a set of code, you are writing directions in a language that the computer can follow. Code is very specific! Without code, computers wouldn't know how to do anything.

conditional statement: A conditional statement is used in code when you need one thing to happen, but only if another does. These are also called *if then* statements. When using this code block, the block at the top is the start of the condition; what you want to happen *if* the first part of the condition is met goes inside the bracket (or the conditional block).

coordinate: An object's exact **X-position** and **Y-position** on a **coordinate plane**. Think of it as a very specific spot!

coordinate plane: A coordinate plane is made up of an X and Y axis. These two axes run perpendicular to each other—one runs up and down, and the other runs right to left. When they meet, the axes create four quadrants. A positive Y coordinate will be in one of the upper quadrants. A negative Y coordinate will be in one of the lower quadrants. A positive X coordinate will be in one of the right quadrants. A negative X coordinate will be in one of the left quadrants.

loop: Loops are used when something needs to happen more than once and can be used with one piece of code or many. The code inside the loop will run (on repeat) in the order it's placed in, just like if it were outside the loop.

origin: The middle point of a coordinate plane. This is where the X-coordinate and Y-coordinate both equal zero and the two axes cross.

parallel processing: When two sets of code are run under the same start command. Think about if you wanted to play a sound and move a sprite at the same time. Since code is run in sequence, if you placed all the code under one start command, the program would play the sound and *then* the sprite would move. To make both things happen at once, you need two different code blocks, each with the same start command. Put the **Sound** block under one and the **Motion** block under another. This way the sound and movement will happen at the same time!

sequence: When something is completed in a specific order. In coding, all programs run in a sequence from top to bottom, meaning the top piece of code will be run first, then the block under it, until the sequence is complete.

sprite: Any movable character or object used in a Scratch project. Sprites can be selected through the Scratch Library, created using drawing tools, or uploaded from the computer.

tempo: The speed of music being played; sometimes referred to as the beat of the music!

user interface: The way a person (or user) interacts with a computer. Basic user interfaces are your computer keyboard or mouse. Makey Makey is another type of user interface!

variable: A variable is a placeholder for a value and can be made in the **Data** category of the Scripts tab. The value of a variable can be changed throughout the course of a project. For example, if a variable was used for the number of lives in a game, you could set it to three at the start of a game. Then each time one sprite touches a certain sprite, the lives variable can be coded to decrease by one.

vector mode: The drawing tools in this mode are similar to tools in bitmap mode. However, in vector mode you can create another shape and still go back to a previous one and move it. In this mode, you can also reshape objects that you have made.

X-axis: The axis that runs horizontally (side to side) in a coordinate plane.

Y-axis: The axis that runs vertically (up and down) in a coordinate plane.

ABOUT THE AUTHOR

Rachel Ziter was raised in Las Vegas, Nevada. She earned a Bachelor of Science in Education and her teaching credentials from Florida Southern College. She has also completed graduate coursework in computer science education at St. Scholastica, as well as professional development in fablab project-based learning at NuVu. Rachel currently works at the Adelson Educational Campus in Las Vegas and is a member of the Tech Team, where she teaches STEM curriculum and instruction, mentors students, and teaches coding and engineering.